For Mom and Dad, who taught three sons the importance of gathering together and giving back, and created so many cherished memories

For our wives, Wendy and Lara, who tirelessly support everything we do

For our children, with whom we continue the tradition of coming together around food. Hannah, Sarah, and Zoë, and Rebecca and Bridget, we hope that one day you will cherish the memories that we are still creating

For all of our friends, over all of the years, with whom we have been so fortunate to join around dining room tables, kitchen counters, restaurant banquettes, picnic tables or on a blanket in a park or on a rocky island

contents

Foreword by Lynn Crawford   1

Peter & Chris Neal   2
Halibut Crunch   6
Enchilada Pie   9

Good Food Is Just the Beginning
Community Food Centres Canada   10

Andrea Carlson   16
Spring Sprouts Hazelnut Gomae   18
Mushroom & Toasted Bran Risotto   21

Andrew George 24
Seafood Chowder 26
Braised Buffalo Ribs with Red Pepper Pesto 29

Ashrafi Ahmed 30
Rainbow Veggie Curry 32
Chingri Malai Curry (Shrimp Curry) 35

Ben Kramer 36
Soft Polenta with Stewed Mushrooms & Parsley Salad 38

Bertrand Alépée   42

Duck Breast with Truffle Jus, Roasted Carrots
   & Parsnip Purée   44

Salted Caramel Millefeuille with Pears
   & Crème Anglaise   49

Brad Long   52

Don Valley Pudding   54

Leek & Oatmeal Biscuits   57

Carl Heinrich   58

Slow-Cooked Trout Bourguignon   60

Caramelized Onion Perogies with Braised
   Beef Shank & Celery Root Purée   65

Chris Brown   68

Bread & Butter Pickles   70

Wild Mushroom & Stinging Nettle Gnocchi   73

Elana Rosenfeld   76

Rocky Mountain Scones   78

Kicking Horse Café's Gluten-Free Cookies   81

Kick Ass French-Press Coffee   82

Gillian Flies — 84

Maple-Glazed Carrots — 86
Sautéed Beet Greens — 89
Roasted Beets — 90

Ian Walker — 92

Blueberry Buckle Cake — 94
Chocolate Cake with Hippie Flakes — 97

Jamie Kennedy — 98

Marinated Wild Sockeye Salmon — 100
Bacon Rösti with Cheesy Scrambled Eggs — 103

Jean-François Archambault — 106

Zesty Guacamole — 108
Salmon Rillettes — 111

Jenn Prager — 112

Turkey Chowder — 114
Macaroni & Cheese — 117

John Lai — 118

Side Ribs Soup — 120
Malaysian Chicken Curry — 123

Joshna Maharaj — 124
Cauliflower Kale Gratin — 126
Quinoa Chicken Salad — 129

Judy Dempsey — 130
Chickpea & Pancetta Soup — 132
Spicy Pork Noodles — 135

Judy Servay — 136
Dahl Soup — 138
Mujaddara — 143

Keith Froggett — 146
Wild Leek & Morel Quiche — 148
Panna Cotta — 151

Kim Fox — 152
Smoky Chakchouka — 154
Burrito Bowl — 157

Kristina McMillan — 160
Baked Pickerel with Mango Salsa — 162
Poached Pears in Red Wine — 165

Lil MacPherson — 166

Roasted Beet, Aged Gouda & Pickled Onion Salad — 168
Savoury Braised Lamb Shanks with Barley Risotto — 173

Liz Anderson — 176

Canadian Cheese Fondue — 178
The Best Gluten-Free Brownies — 181

Lora Kirk — 182

Crispy Egg & Pork Belly Salad with Green
   Goddess Dressing — 184
Ginger Stout Cake with Orange Meringue
   & Coffee Caramel — 189

Michael Ableman — 192

Grilled Radicchio with Balsamic Vinegar — 194
Winter Root Mash — 197

Mike Fata — 198

Spicy Hemp Hummus — 200
Hemp Granola Bars — 203

Miriam Streiman — 204

Caramel Apple Butter — 206
Caramel Apple Butter Rugelach — 209

Ned Bell — 212
Dungeness Crab Tacos — 214
BC Albacore Tuna with "Pickled" Haskap Berries — 219

Nick Saul — 222
Root Vegetable Slaw — 224
Pots de Crème — 227

Paul Rogalski — 228
Roasted Cauliflower & Parsnip Soup — 230
Tangled Beef Flank in Sherry Vinaigrette — 233

Paul Taylor — 236
Roasted Potato Salad — 238
Juicy Chicken Sandwich — 241

Rocco Agostino — 242
Beet Caprese — 244
Arancini with Mozzarella — 247

Sarah Harmer — 250
Savoury Veggie Pie — 252
Squash Pesto Feta Bake — 257

Scott MacNeil — 258

Easiest Summer Tomato Tart — 260

Grilled Skirt Steak with Grilled Asparagus
& Burdock Root Purée — 263

Sharon Hapton — 266

Potato Leek Soup — 268

Chicken Creole with Ancient Grains — 271

Todd Perrin — 272

House Ketchup — 274

Rum BBQ Sauce — 277

Baked Beans — 278

Vikram Vij — 280

Sautéed Spinach & Tomatoes with Quinoa & Paneer — 282

Butter Chicken Schnitzel — 285

Where to Find the Goodness — 290

Acknowledgements — 292

Credits — 294

Index — 296

recipes

Breakfast

Kick Ass French-Press Coffee	82
Bacon Rösti with Cheesy Scrambled Eggs	103
Wild Leek & Morel Quiche	148
Smoky Chakchouka	154
Hemp Granola Bars	203

Soups

Seafood Chowder	26
Turkey Chowder	114
Side Ribs Soup	120
Chickpea & Pancetta Soup	132
Dahl Soup	138
Roasted Cauliflower & Parsnip Soup	230
Potato Leek Soup	268
Chicken Creole with Ancient Grains	271

Salads & Dressings

Spring Sprouts Hazelnut Gomae	18
Quinoa Chicken Salad	129
Roasted Beet, Aged Gouda & Pickled Onion Salad	168
Crispy Egg & Pork Belly Salad with Green Goddess Dressing	184
Root Vegetable Slaw	224
Roasted Potato Salad	238
Beet Caprese	244

Appetizers & Small Plates

Don Valley Pudding	54
Marinated Wild Sockeye Salmon	100
Arancini with Mozzarella	247
Easiest Summer Tomato Tart	260

Sides

Maple-Glazed Carrots	86
Sautéed Beet Greens	89
Roasted Beets	90
Cauliflower Kale Gratin	126
Mujaddara	143
Grilled Radicchio with Balsamic Vinegar	194
Winter Root Mash	197
Baked Beans	278
Sautéed Spinach & Tomatoes with Quinoa & Paneer	282

Mains

Veggies

Rainbow Veggie Curry	32
Soft Polenta with Stewed Mushrooms & Parsley Salad	38
Savoury Veggie Pie	252
Squash Pesto Feta Bake	257

Pasta & Rice

Mushroom & Toasted Bran Risotto	21
Wild Mushroom & Stinging Nettle Gnocchi	73
Macaroni & Cheese	117

Fish & Seafood

Halibut Crunch	6
Chingri Malai Curry (Shrimp Curry)	35
Slow-Cooked Trout Bourguignon	60
Baked Pickerel with Mango Salsa	162
Dungeness Crab Tacos	214
BC Albacore Tuna with "Pickled" Haskap Berries	219

Chicken & Fowl

Enchilada Pie	9
Duck Breast with Truffle Jus, Roasted Carrots & Parsnip Purée	44
Malaysian Chicken Curry	123
Juicy Chicken Sandwich	241
Butter Chicken Schnitzel	285

Beef, Lamb & Pork

Braised Buffalo Ribs with Red Pepper Pesto 29

Caramelized Onion Perogies with Braised
    Beef Shank & Celery Root Purée 65

Spicy Pork Noodles 135

Burrito Bowl 157

Savoury Braised Lamb Shanks with Barley Risotto 173

Tangled Beef Flank in Sherry Vinaigrette 233

Grilled Skirt Steak with Grilled Asparagus 263
    & Burdock Root Purée

Dips & Spreads

Zesty Guacamole 108

Salmon Rillettes 111

Canadian Cheese Fondue 178

Spicy Hemp Hummus 200

Caramel Apple Butter 206

Sauces & Condiments

Bread & Butter Pickles 70

House Ketchup 274

Rum BBQ Sauce 277

Baked Goods

Leek & Oatmeal Biscuits   57

Rocky Mountain Scones   78

Kicking Horse Café's Gluten-Free Cookies   81

Blueberry Buckle Cake   94

The Best Gluten-Free Brownies   181

Caramel Apple Butter Rugelach   209

Desserts

Salted Caramel Millefeuille with Pears
    & Crème Anglaise   49

Chocolate Cake with Hippie Flakes   97

Panna Cotta   151

Poached Pears in Red Wine   165

Ginger Stout Cake with Orange Meringue
    & Coffee Caramel   189

Pots de Crème   227

foreword

Lynn Crawford

For me, cooking at home involves lots of laughter, family, and friends. I treasure the moments when we come together to share good food, cultivating family traditions and creating lasting memories. These moments have formed the cornerstones of my cooking philosophy, and I believe that many Canadians feel the same way. It's reflected in the current movement to return to our roots by using fresh ingredients that have been locally grown, raised, and harvested.

It is that act of sharing a good meal prepared with care that Peter and Chris Neal celebrate in this book. *Goodness* is a sublime collection of stories and recipes that shines a light on the many talented chefs, growers, entrepreneurs, and food fighters across Canada who not only share their passion for good, local food but act on their beliefs that the very same good food should be accessible to all.

To that end, these individuals, many of whom I know and have worked with, have donated the recipes in this book to support Community Food Centres Canada (CFCC). I am proud to say that 50% of the profits from the sale of this amazing book will be given to CFCC to help them continue to "grow, cook, share, and advocate for healthy food for all." I know you will find a recipe that will spark your passion and increase your appetite for fresh, locally grown food and inspire you to set the table and share the goodness in your community.

Peter & Chris Neal

Co-owners
Neal Brothers Foods Inc.
Concord, ON

Hometown: Aurora, ON

We were fortunate enough to grow up in a household where we routinely gathered as a family at dinnertime. Back then we never realized what the simple act of eating a meal together every day would come to mean to us, but they were amazing times. Friends who were asked to join our table and did, sometimes sheepishly, have in subsequent years confessed to how thrilled they were to partake and remember those days fondly. We talked, we laughed, we cried, we listened, we joked while together we enjoyed the simple, good food our mom prepared for us. Ours was a table that welcomed so many and where so many felt at home and part of the family, and that's a tradition we are now trying to carry forward with our families.

Growing up, our parents also instilled in us a desire to contribute and be active participants in our community. They set a strong example by regularly volunteering for church events and always being the first ones to say yes whenever help was needed. When the beautiful, historic buildings along Main Street in Unionville were at risk of being demolished, our family was at the forefront fighting for their preservation—and succeeded.

These memories have helped to shape our feelings around food and community, and certainly our philosophy when it comes to our business, Neal Brothers Foods.

Neal Brothers Foods had its humble start in 1988 in our parents' kitchen in Aurora, Ontario. At that time, consumers were becoming more conscious about healthy food choices and salads had become quite popular (it's also when mesclun salad mixes first burst onto the scene). Subsequently, the gourmet food industry was growing. Inspired by some gourmet potato chips we had tried on a road trip through the US during university, we decided we wanted to enter the food business. After some brainstorming, we thought of croutons. We knew we could offer a better alternative to the salad accompaniments on the market. Croutons Croûtons, handmade preservative-free seasoned croutons, was our first product, and to our delight and relief—we had sold Chris's prized hockey card collection for $800 to fund our new business—it was a hit.

The first Neal Brothers product.

It soon became clear that we were on to something consumers really liked: a great-tasting product made with local ingredients whenever possible and a lot of care. Knowing there was a demand and fuelled by our early success, we decided to turn our efforts to product development and distribution.

We launched a line of tortilla chips and salsas, including our 100% stone-ground organic blue-corn tortilla chips. At first getting the blue chips into stores was tough going. Back then the blue chips were a bit too adventurous for both retailers and consumers. Some people thought that we dyed them, while others thought they looked burnt. Only a few health food stores in downtown Toronto would sell them, but we believed in them and stuck to it, and they are now one of our best-selling products.

It's been over 25 years, and we're so proud of what we have accomplished and to have witnessed the increasing desire for good, natural, healthy food. Ingredients like coconut oil and flaxseeds, which seemed alien just 10 years ago, are now commonplace. Organics have earned prime shelf space. People seek out GMO-free products. We've made it our business to source not just the best ingredients, but also, whenever possible, those grown locally with organics and sustainability top of mind, and in doing so we've built a network of like-minded growers and suppliers. More than 70% of the 50 products we produce and distribute are non-GMO and 50% are organic. It's important for us

Peter and Chris making croutons in the early days.

Peter and Chris, then and now, with wives Lara and Wendy.

Some of the 50 products we distribute.

to align ourselves with businesses that choose goodness—both in the quality of their products and for their communities and the planet.

We don't have a playbook on how to conduct our business. Each and every day we simply try to make decisions that we can feel good about. We're okay with foregoing sales in favour of staying true to our beliefs, and we won't sell our products through multinational chains that don't treat their employees with fairness and dignity. It just doesn't make sense to us.

When we were taking our first baby steps into the specialty food realm we were so fortunate to receive support from some pretty awesome people. Our parents and friends would peel garlic for our croutons until their fingers burned. Mentors kindly offered us—two fresh-faced rookies (ages 20 and 22)—sage advice to help us grow our burgeoning company. That generosity of spirit is not something we have forgotten, and we like to pay it forward. Over the last 10 years, Peter has mentored over 100 young professionals trying to start their own businesses. We have also supported a vast array of fantastic organizations, including Camp Oochigeas, Young People's Theatre, Big Brothers Big Sisters Canada, Juvenile Diabetes Research Foundation, and many other not-for-profits and charity events big and small.

Giving back has become a core principle of our business, and we are always looking for ways to contribute and make a difference. When friends mentioned a local organization in Toronto called The Stop, we were intrigued. The Stop was taking the traditional food bank model and standing it on its ear, creating a dignified space where people could come together to eat, learn, share, and take an active role in shaping their neighbourhood. These things resonated with us. We met Nick Saul, toured their facilities, and learned more about what they were doing. The Stop was (and still is) an incredible place

 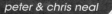

that offered everything from urban gardening to meal programs, cooking classes, and community ovens. We knew that we wanted to get involved.

We donated food and attended fundraisers. It became even clearer to us: good food has the power to enrich lives and build strong communities. As The Stop grew and became part of Community Food Centres Canada (CFCC), an organization with a nationwide focus, we became members of their national advisory board.

During a 2014 national advisory council meeting for the CFCC, members were challenged with raising awareness and funds. We had a light bulb moment: What if we Neal Brothers could produce a cookbook that shone a light on philanthropy and entrepreneurship to inspire people as well as educate them about CFCC? If successful, we could raise funds at the same time.

It just made so much sense we couldn't not do it. We got to work talking to our network of good food fighters, who introduced us to other people doing good, and before long we had a list of 37 incredible people from across Canada doing amazing things and making a difference in their communities, all of them eager to donate their time and recipes to help raise money for Community Food Centres Canada. *Goodness: Recipes & Stories* was born.

Peter, Nick Saul, and Chris at the Grow for The Stop fundraiser at The New Farm, 2015.

More than just a collection of recipes, *Goodness* is a celebration of good food and dynamic people who demonstrate on a daily basis that goodness matters. It's our hope that not only will you enjoy the incredible range of delicious recipes captured between these pages, but that you will read the stories and feel inspired to make a difference in your own community, whether that be by simply taking the time to eat together with family, friends, and neighbours or reaching further into your community to participate in local events or even organizing your own community events to raise money for the things that matter to you. And we also hope that you'll learn more about Community Food Centres Canada, the amazing work they do, and how you can get involved and make a difference. In whatever ways make sense to you, we hope you will…

#spreadgoodness

Adding a crispy topping of crushed potato chips is an easy way to dress up fish and make it more enticing—our kids actually request fish for dinner because they love it so much! Served with a side salad, this dish makes an easy mid-week meal or a casual weekend dinner with friends. Make it your own by using your favourite flavours of mayo and potato chips!

halibut crunch

serves 4

2 ½ cups potato chips (we prefer Neal Brothers Srirachup Kettle Chips)

2 heaping tbsp spicy mayonnaise (we prefer Neal Brothers Sriracha Mayonnaise)

4 halibut fillets, skin-on (4 to 6 ounces each)

Chopped fresh flat-leaf parsley leaves (optional)

1 Preheat the oven to 350°F. Line a baking sheet with parchment paper.

2 Place potato chips in a food processor fitted with the metal blade and process until they resemble coarse bread crumbs. (Alternatively, crush them right in the opened bag using a rolling pin.)

3 Place fish on the prepared baking sheet. Spread mayonnaise evenly overtop. Coat fish in chip crumbs (only the top of the fish), pressing lightly so they stick to the mayo.

4 Bake in the preheated oven for about 20 minutes, until coating is crispy and golden brown and fish is opaque and flakes easily with a fork. Garnish with parsley, if using.

· tips ·

If you like, substitute an equal amount of salmon or chicken for the halibut.

Experiment using your favourite varieties of Neal Brothers mayonnaise and potato chips—for example, Lime Mayonnaise and Vij's Delhi-licious Kettle Chips.

Our girls are not big beef fans so this easy Mexican-inspired dish
is a nice alternative. It makes a perfect mid-week family meal. It can
also be made ahead and frozen, which makes it perfect for taking up
to the cottage. Serve with sour cream and garnish with chopped
fresh cilantro or parsley, if desired (though we just eat it as is).

enchilada pie

serves 6 to 8

1 lb lean ground turkey

2 tsp ground cumin

2 cups salsa (we prefer Neal Brothers Corn Salsa)

1 cup frozen corn kernels

3 large (12-inch) flour tortillas

1 cup shredded cheese (we prefer Mexican blend or mozzarella)

1 Preheat the oven to 350°F. Grease a deep-dish pie plate or a casserole dish large enough to fit tortillas when laid flat.

2 In a skillet over medium heat, combine ground turkey and cumin. Cook, stirring to break up any clumps, for about 5 minutes or until meat is no longer pink.

3 Stir in salsa and corn. Bring mixture to a simmer and cook for about 10 minutes to let the flavours meld. Remove from heat.

4 Place 1 tortilla in the bottom of the prepared baking dish. Spread with half of the turkey mixture. Sprinkle with one-third of the cheese. Top with second tortilla. Cover with remaining turkey mixture and sprinkle with another third of the cheese. Top with remaining tortilla (reserve remaining cheese). Cover the baking dish with aluminum foil. Bake in the preheated oven for 30 minutes.

5 Sprinkle with remaining cheese and bake, uncovered, for another 10 minutes, or until cheese melts. Let cool 5 to 10 minutes before serving. Garnish with chopped fresh parsley or cilantro or sour cream, if desired.

Good Food Is Just the Beginning

Community Food Centres Canada

Food is this incredible thing. If you eat it together, you grow community and connection. Through it you can express your culture and your background. If you eat good food, it energizes you and keeps you healthy. When you grow food sustainably, it nourishes the soil and increases the health of our planet. And when everyone has access to good food, you have inclusive, connected, and equitable communities.

These words from Nick Saul, president and CEO of Community Food Centres Canada (CFCC), explain not only the power of food but also the cornerstones on which CFCC was built and operates.

As a society, we're increasingly aware of the impact our food choices have on our health and well-being. At the same time, we're faced with the fact that we've lost many of the basic food skills that form the foundation of healthy eating. The problem is worse for people living on incomes that are too low to allow them to choose the foods they know are best for themselves and their families. Four million Canadians are food insecure, unsure some days of where their next meal is coming from. Many of those affected are children. And research shows that food insecurity is tightly linked to poorer health and higher incidences of diet-related illnesses such as type 2 diabetes and other chronic conditions. The sad truth is that while the availability of high-quality,

Community dinner at The Local Community Food Centre in Stratford, ON.

ethical foods may be increasing, not everyone has access—people who are poor are increasingly being pushed away from the table. It's a big problem that requires large-scale solutions; people—you!—need to call for good policies that can raise incomes and the standard of living for everyone. Canada also needs a visionary national organization that can work to create positive spaces around healthy food and rally Canadians around pushing for equal access for all. That's what Community Food Centres Canada is trying to do.

Neighbours prepare a meal together in The Local's Cook-Ahead Program.

Community Food Centres Canada works to create and support vibrant spaces that bring people together to grow, cook, share, and advocate for healthy food for all. These include Community Food Centres. What is a Community Food Centre? It's a welcoming and dignified place where people can come together around a delicious free meal prepared with care. A place where people can learn cooking and gardening skills, and kids can get their hands dirty in the garden and kitchen in ways that expand their taste buds and teach them how to make healthy food choices. Community Food Centres provide peer support to those in need, and engage community members to become active on issues that affect their lives. Simply put, a Community Food Centre is a place that uses food as a vehicle for people to become part of something larger—an engaged and healthy community.

For most people, the journey to a Community Food Centre begins because of an immediate food need. Food access programs like nutritious community meals, healthy hampers, and affordable produce markets strive to meet the needs of people struggling with food insecurity in a welcoming and respectful environment that

The Stop Community Food Centre's gardening programs grow produce, skills, and friendships.

Kids pick herbs to include in their snack in The Table Community Food Centre's after-school program.

promotes healthy eating and encourages new friend-ships and support. By focusing on sourcing local, sea-sonal ingredients wherever possible, these programs also support the local food economy.

It doesn't end there. During these programs, people can also visit on-site peer advocacy offices staffed by trained community members who can help them access housing, legal, income, and other supports; join a cooking group or enroll their kids in a food-focused after-school program; or start volunteering in the garden. Programs like FoodFit aim to make healthy eating easier by providing practical food skills and nutrition knowledge that help people navigate the dozens of food choices they face every day, and to give participants simple, useful tools that can support them to maximize the control they can take over their health within the limits of their circumstances. Community action training empowers people with lived history of poverty and marginalization to use their experiences to help others who are struggling and to speak out about the challenges they face.

Quickly, good food turns into a pathway to engagement and empowerment.

The Community Food Centre model was developed at The Stop Community Food Centre in Toronto, ON, a place that seeks not only to meet the basic food needs of its community, but also to combat social isolation and stig-matization. The initial success of The Stop and interest in the Community Food Centre model from organizations across Canada led to a pilot expansion phase that saw the opening of The Table Community Food Centre in Perth, ON, in early 2012 and The Local Community Food Centre in Stratford, ON, later that year. Community Food Centres Canada was incorporated in 2012 to work

Peer advocates at the Regent Park Community Food Centre support neighbours in need.

with partners to build more Community Food Centres across Canada. As of summer 2015, there were eight established or developing Community Food Centres—you'll read stories about them in the pages of this book—and a push is underway to build four more in the coming years.

CFCC also works with 75 Good Food Organizations across the country, supporting them to offer health- and equity-building programs through trainings, resources, a grants program, and networking opportunities. The common bond all these organizations share is a belief that healthy food is a basic human right, and a powerful way to build health and hope, skills and community.

NorWest Co-op Community Food Centre's Filipino Family Cooking Group spices up the cold Winnipeg winters.

If you're reading this book, you're probably very familiar with the magical power a good meal has to bring people together. In many ways, this book is just like a good meal—it gathers Canadians from different backgrounds, cities, and cultures to share what good food means to them. That's a really powerful thing—and it's exactly what we need to do in order to make lasting, positive change in our food system. Chefs, farmers, musicians, backyard gardeners, activists, health professionals, good food companies, home cooks—we all need to work together to build a movement that can make equal access to healthy food—food that's good for our health *and* for our planet—a reality in Canada. We know it's within our reach. And we need your help to keep moving.

When everyone has access to good food, you have inclusive, connected, and equitable communities.

We invite you to enjoy and share this book with friends, family, colleagues, and neighbours, and then to join us in the fight for good food for all.

Goodness is the only investment that never fails.

Henry David Thoreau

Andrea Carlson

Chef & co-owner
· Burdock & Co. ·
Vancouver, BC

Hometown: Toronto, ON

Andrea Carlson has been a chef for over 20 years. It has shaped her into a zealous cheerleader for all things local and made her a champion of sustainable seafood and an ardent supporter of her community. How does she thank all the chefs, farmers, fishers, and suppliers who have so generously shared their expertise with her over the years? Andrea likes to pay it forward and teach others how to create more goodness in the world.

In addition to standing behind the stove at her restaurant, Burdock & Co., and running Harvest Community Foods, a grocery and noodle shop with a CSA (community-supported agriculture) program, Andrea is dedicated to working with various non-profit organizations to influence young minds and future generations of chefs.

Andrea serves on the board of directors of Growing Chefs! Chefs for Children's Urban Agriculture, a classroom program that gives students in grades two and three hands-on experience growing and cooking their own food so that they can learn about healthy eating and sustainable food systems.

"It's exciting to see the kids make the connection between growing food, harvesting it, and turning it into something they can eat," she says. "We teach them what's beyond what they see at supermarkets. You can see them get turned on by trying local vegetables and expanding their food knowledge."

Grown-ups too are benefiting from Andrea's flair for educating. She sits on the board of the Chefs' Table Society of BC, a chef-run organization that promotes the exchange of information among the province's culinary talents, and also nurtures up-and-coming professionals with bursaries. As co-chair of the Sustainability/Growers/Green Initiatives Committee, she can highlight the agenda of initiatives like Ocean Wise, launched by the Vancouver Aquarium to promote sustainable seafood. "It's a pressing issue," she explains, "but we still see tiger prawns and sea bass on menus. You still get people using them, despite what we know about how they are caught and the problems with over-fishing. There is so much potential for positive change."

Andrea's education in sustainability and locally grown food came courtesy of the Sooke Harbour House on Vancouver Island, where she worked as a young chef. Raised in Toronto, Andrea was in awe of the wealth of ingredients on the island that were available for her to cook with. While tending the inn's garden, she learned about edible flowers and herbs; she was also introduced to forag-ing the bounty of ingredients the surrounding area offered.

"It was the first time I had worked in a place that used that kind of produce," she recalls. "My path for what kind of chef I wanted to be was set. I got so much inspiration from the owners, Frederique and Sinclair. It was life-changing."

That experience motivated Andrea to make the move to Raincity Grill in Van-couver in 1992, the first Canadian restaurant to feature a menu based exclusively on the 100-mile diet, and then to the iconic Bishop's restaurant (she left in 2012). Andrea now shares her love of local at her own restaurant, Burdock & Co.

"We try hard not to be preachy," she says. "You don't want to be shoving information down people's throats. We want people to come here and enjoy themselves, but there are still many opportunities to share information."

Perhaps the greatest irony is that Andrea didn't grow up eating healthy food. She admits that as a teen her diet was heavy on packaged foods. She had to learn what not to eat. The shift came when her family got a copy of Craig Claiborne's *The New York Times Cook Book*. From it, she learned how to make chicken parmigiana. Later came chocolate mousse, courtesy of Julia Child. She discovered she had a natural talent for cooking, and her parents would ask her to cook when friends came over. Once Andrea learned she could educate palates through food, she was hooked.

> *Being part of a community means being able to support what you believe in.*

 andrea carlson

A *gomae* is a Japanese side dish traditionally made with steamed greens topped with a sesame dressing. In this version, we swap out the sesame seeds for roasted hazelnuts (Canadian Hazelnut in Agassiz, BC, supplies us with fresh nuts) and use a mix of fresh springtime greens, such as sunflower and pea shoots, spinach, and kale tips (we get ours from Urban Food Peddlers, who deliver fresh veg by bicycle).

spring sprouts hazelnut gomae

serves 4

1 cup roasted hazelnuts, divided (see Tips)

1 cup grapeseed oil

¼ cup cider vinegar (we prefer Spectrum brand)

¼ cup pure maple syrup, liquid honey, or mirin

¼ cup soy sauce (we prefer gluten-free)

¼ cup tahini

Sea salt

4 cups mixed greens (see Tips)

1 Using a pestle and mortar, crush 4 tbsp hazelnuts for garnish and set aside.

2 In a blender, combine remaining hazelnuts, grapeseed oil, vinegar, maple syrup, soy sauce, tahini, and salt to taste. Blend on high speed until smooth.

3 Divide mixed greens among serving plates. Drizzle with prepared dressing. Top with reserved crushed hazelnuts. Serve.

tips

To roast hazelnuts, place them in a dry skillet over medium heat and cook, stirring constantly, for 5 to 7 minutes, until fragrant and browned.

We like to use sunflower sprouts, asparagus tips, baby kale, and blanched fiddleheads in this salad.

To blanch fiddleheads, add them to a saucepan of boiling water and cook for 2 minutes, or until bright green. Drain well.

This is a simple, clean risotto that lets the nuttiness of the toasted bran and the sweetness of the rice shine through. We like to use rice produced by Masa Shiroki—it's the first rice grown in BC!

mushroom & toasted bran risotto

serves 2

7 tbsp butter, divided

2 shallots, finely diced

1½ cups risotto rice (see Tip)

¼ cup dry white wine

3 to 4 cups hot water, divided

Sea salt

4 tbsp toasted rice bran (see Tips, p. 22)

½ cup black trumpet mushrooms, roughly chopped (see Tips, p. 22)

3 oz shaved aged farmhouse cheese (we prefer fermiere)

Sour Bran Broth (optional; recipe follows)

1 In a skillet over medium heat, melt 4 tbsp butter. Add shallots and cook for 2 to 3 minutes, stirring occasionally, until softened.

2 Add rice and cook, stirring often, for 2 minutes, until well coated. Add wine and cook, stirring to scrape up any browned bits from the bottom of the pan, until wine has almost evaporated, about 1 minute.

3 Add 1 cup hot water, stirring constantly until absorbed by rice, about 5 minutes. Add remaining hot water 1 cup at a time, continuing to stir constantly until rice is creamy yet slightly firm (al dente).

4 Sprinkle with salt to taste. Stir in 2 tbsp butter and toasted rice bran. Cover and set aside, keeping warm.

5 In a clean skillet, melt remaining 1 tbsp butter. Add mushrooms and cook until softened, 4 to 5 minutes.

6 Divide risotto among serving bowls. Top with sautéed mushrooms, cheese, and sour bran broth (if using). Serve.

· *tip* ·

The best types of rice for risotto are Italian short-grain varieties, which provide the right amount of starch to achieve a creamy result. If you can't find Agassiz-grown rice, arborio and carnaroli are both good choices.

continued…

sour bran broth

If you are feeling adventurous and have the time, make this tasty broth to finish the risotto.

⅓ cup water, at room temperature

2 tbsp rice bran

Pinch sea salt

1 In a glass jar, combine water, rice bran, and salt and stir well.

2 Cover mouth of jar with cheesecloth and set aside in a dark, cool place for 2 days to ferment.

3 Carefully strain liquid through the cheesecloth into a small saucepan (discard solids). Season with salt and pepper to taste.

4 Just before serving, warm over medium heat. Spoon a couple of tablespoons around the edge of each bowl of rice.

· tips ·

To toast rice bran, place it in a dry pan over medium heat and heat, stirring often, for about 3 minutes, until it smells nutty.

If you can't find black trumpet mushrooms (also known as black chanterelles), you can substitute an equal quantity of almost any other type of wild mushroom, such as pines, chanterelles, or cauliflower mushrooms.

*Goodness is the outcome
of giving and/or receiving
the best of anything and
everything.*

*Mary & Stan Neal
(Mom & Dad)*

Andrew George

Chef & educator
Vancouver, BC

Hometown: Smithers, BC

Education is a path to all good things. Accomplished chef Andrew George is living proof of that. He has gone from living in the tiny village of Telkwa, BC (population less than 500), to discovering the world, from Frankfurt to New Orleans, as Canada's most beloved ambassador for First Nations cuisine. Andrew's love of learning has made it possible for him to accomplish so much. Throughout his career, he has been spreading the word to young people, especially Aboriginal youths, about the wealth of opportunities that await them when pursuing a career as a chef.

In 1992, when Andrew participated in the World Culinary Olympics in Germany, he was struck by the absence of indigenous people at the competition. "I kept wondering, 'Where are our people?' Cooking is a wonderful career that has been so great to me. I could not understand why they weren't getting involved. That was the moment I realized that I had to show them the many opportunities available."

True to his vision, Andrew has spent several years being a teacher and mentor to many. He has lectured about the hospitality industry at colleges and universities across Canada, talked to elementary and high-school students about the joys of becoming a chef, and led a program at the Kla-how-eya Aboriginal Centre in North Surrey and other organizations that saw several hundred students go through pre-apprenticeship and professional cook (level 1) programs—many of whom went on to other institutes to further their culinary journeys. "It's like watching your kids grow up," says Andrew. "It makes you a little nervous, them moving on, but also very proud at the same time."

Andrew enjoys the leadership role he's taken with the many organizations he works with, including SuperChefs of the Universe, a non-profit organization that offers programs such as Cookery for Kids in Surrey, BC. The one-day sessions were created to empower children in the battle against childhood obesity by getting them into the kitchen with chefs like Andrew to learn about balanced nutrition and food preparation.

"A lot of people tell kids how to cook and eat, but no one actually shows them," he says. "We actually do that, and the kids just love it." Class alumni go on to do cooking demos for other kids at events and schools in order to inspire them to become healthy too. Andrew saw one of his students ultimately lose 80 pounds and be chosen to represent SuperChefs at events all over North America.

If Andrew is not spending his time developing menus, cooking at big events, or serving as an apprentice adviser to the BC government, he's doing outreach in Aboriginal communities. He wants to see them flourish and excel. He connects their struggles to hunger: "What it boils down to, in my opinion, is a lack of food. When you go to school, you can't learn without something good and nutritious in your stomach. It affects your confidence, and it snowballs from there."

> *I tell Aboriginal youths that they have to go and seek out opportunities. "Get educated, then come back to teach what you've learned to others and build stronger communities."*

At this point in his career, Andrew wants to focus on igniting a passion for cooking and learning in others. "I've accomplished everything I wanted to. I've been there and done that," he says, laughing. "I became a cook, then a chef; ran a restaurant and owned one; wrote some books; became an instructor and travelled the world. I'm giving it back now. I'm setting the table for the next generation. I want other Aboriginal cooks to experience the rewards that come with doing something you love. It will change their lives, just as it changed mine."

25 *andrew george*

A version of this rich and delicious chowder was a favourite
with customers at my Toody Ni Grill in Vancouver.

seafood chowder

serves 6 to 8

8 cups fish stock or water

½ cup bacon fat or butter

1 onion, diced

1 rib celery, diced

4 cloves garlic, crushed

1 bay leaf

1 cup dry white wine

½ cup all-purpose flour

1 large potato, diced

1 medium carrot, diced

½ green bell pepper,
seeded and diced

⅓ lb fresh clams

⅓ lb skinless, boneless
salmon, cubed

⅓ lb skinless, boneless
red snapper, cubed

Sea salt and freshly ground
black pepper

½ cup whipping (35%) cream

2 tbsp chopped fresh dill

2 tbsp chopped fresh flat-leaf
parsley leaves

1 In a large saucepan, bring stock to a boil.

2 Meanwhile, in a large heavy soup pot over medium-high heat, warm bacon fat. Add onion, celery, garlic, and bay leaf and sauté until onion is translucent, 3 to 4 minutes.

3 Add wine and cook, stirring to scrape up any browned bits from the bottom of the pan, until liquid is reduced by half, about 5 minutes.

4 Add flour and cook, stirring constantly, until a thick paste (a roux) forms, about 2 minutes.

5 Slowly add hot stock to roux, stirring well to prevent lumps. Bring to a simmer.

6 Add potato, carrot, and green pepper; simmer until vegetables are tender, about 5 minutes.

7 Add clams, salmon, and red snapper. Reduce heat to low and cook until fish is cooked through and tender, about 10 minutes. Discard bay leaf and any clams that have not opened. Season with salt and pepper to taste.

8 Remove from heat and stir in just enough cream to turn chowder white.

9 Just before serving, stir in fresh herbs.

I developed this recipe for my students as part of a lesson about the different sauces and braising methods used for cooking ribs. It's a delicious exercise.

braised buffalo ribs
with red pepper pesto

serves 4

3 lb buffalo ribs

Freshly cracked black pepper

4 tbsp vegetable oil, divided

2 cups diced tomatoes, with juice

½ cup red pepper pesto

½ cup dark ale

¼ cup soy sauce

2 tbsp packed brown sugar

6 cloves garlic, crushed

1 Preheat the oven to 325°F.

2 Pat dry buffalo ribs with paper towel. Season with pepper to taste.

3 In a large heavy-bottomed or cast-iron skillet over medium-high heat, heat 2 tbsp oil. Add ribs and cook for about 5 minutes per side, until browned. Remove the pan from heat and transfer ribs to a roasting pan. Set aside.

4 In a bowl, combine tomatoes, red pepper pesto, ale, soy sauce, brown sugar, remaining 2 tbsp oil, and garlic. Pour over browned ribs.

5 Transfer the roasting pan to the preheated oven. Roast for 3 hours, basting ribs with sauce every 30 minutes, or until meat is very tender and begins to fall off the bone when pulled with a fork. Serve.

Ashrafi Ahmed

Community gardens coordinator
Regent Park Community Food Centre
Toronto, ON

Hometown: Dhaka, Bangladesh, IN

More than a decade ago, Ashrafi Ahmed, along with her husband and 15-month-old son, arrived in Canada from Bangladesh. She was two months pregnant. They had left everything behind—their jobs, family, and friends—to seek out a better life. Establishing themselves in a country where everything, from the languages to the customs, was totally unfamiliar was difficult, but that didn't stop Ashrafi from jumping in feet first to support her new community.

"When I came to Canada, I wanted a new identity," she says. "I didn't want to just do the usual housewife things … I thought if I volunteered, I could learn so much—like languages. Sometimes I feel shy with people because I think they can't understand me. But when I started volunteering, many people helped me with my English and gave me encouragement. I realized that Canada is a really good place."

Over the years, Ashrafi has worked with various organizations, including the Regent Park Community Health Centre, where she served as a liaison between staff and those seeking medical help, interpreting and offering encouragement. She could see the difference her support made: clients felt more comfortable when they had her by their side.

Now employed full time at the Regent Park Community Food Centre—which launched in 2014 through a partnership between Community Food Centres Canada and CRC—Ashrafi, with her innate gift for nurturing, friendly manner, and genuine warmth, is a go-to person in the community. "This place is my home," she says. "People share so much with me. I love them and they love me. We are like one big family."

The participants of our community meals say the food tastes better here. I know why. All the recipes include an extra ingredient—love.

"As soon as I started here, I felt like I belonged," explains Ashrafi. "I like the centre's goals and mission to serve the community, to help people who don't have adequate access to food or space for gardening. It has everything, including community advocates and counselling about housing."

As the centre's garden coordinator, Ashrafi leads programs on a variety of topics, such as composting, container gardening, seed germination, and disease prevention, along with assisting participants with their community garden plots. The programs are designed to improve access to good food using a hands-on approach. Ashrafi notices immediate benefits of the gardens as well: "They are a good place to form friendships with other gardeners. People come together to share their experiences and knowledge from different cultures and to grow their own food. That all helps build a stronger community."

Ashrafi loves seeing the excitement on the faces of the gardeners when they harvest their first vegetables. She'll often hear, "Wow! I grew this!" She recounts the time a little girl, not yet even two years old, shyly asked if she could have a tomato. "She was so thrilled. It was like she had been given the best present ever. Now, when she sees me, she points and yells, 'Tomato!' It brings tears of joy to my eyes."

 ashrafi ahmed

This rich and healthy squash curry is a wonderful main dish. Don't let the ingredients list faze you; this really is an easy dish to make. Serve over rice or roti.

rainbow veggie curry

serves 6 to 10

¼ cup + 1 tbsp vegetable oil, divided

2 tbsp minced onion, divided

½ tsp ground turmeric

½ tsp chili powder

½ tsp ground coriander

½ tsp ground cumin

½ tsp ginger paste

¼ tsp garlic paste

Sea salt

2 chayote squash, peeled and cubed

1 butternut squash, peeled and cubed

2 potatoes, peeled and cubed

1 sweet potato, peeled and cubed

2 tsp milk

1 cup water

2 green chiles, seeded and sliced

1 tsp panchforan spice mix (see Tip)

1 tbsp chopped fresh cilantro leaves

1 In a large saucepan over medium heat, heat 1 tbsp oil. Add 1 tbsp of the onion and cook until browned, 3 to 4 minutes.

2 Stir in turmeric, chili powder, coriander, cumin, ginger paste, and garlic paste; cook until fragrant, about 1 minute. Season with salt to taste.

3 Add squashes and potatoes and stir to coat well.

4 Add milk and water. Cover and cook for 15 to 20 minutes, until vegetables are tender.

5 Meanwhile, in a skillet over high heat, heat remaining ¼ cup oil. Stir in chiles, panchforan, and remaining 1 tbsp onion and sauté until onion is browned, 3 to 4 minutes. Add to vegetables and stir gently until incorporated.

6 To serve, divide among serving bowls and garnish with cilantro.

· tip ·

Panchforan is a whole spice blend that includes cumin, brown mustard seed, fenugreek, nigella seed, and fennel seed. You can find it in well-stocked grocers or Indian markets.

The Hindi word *malai* means "cream," but this delicious, mild curry gets its creaminess from coconut milk. It's a very popular dish in Bangladesh, and I love to cook it for my family. Serve with jasmine rice.

chingri malai curry (shrimp curry)

serves 4 to 6

1 tbsp vegetable oil

2 onions, chopped

14 oz large shrimp, peeled and deveined, tail removed

Sea salt

½ tsp ground turmeric

½ tsp chili powder

½ tsp ground cumin

½ tsp ginger paste (see Tips)

3 tbsp coconut milk powder (see Tips)

2 tbsp water

½ tsp tomato paste

2 whole green chiles

1 In a deep skillet over medium heat, heat oil. Add onions and shrimp and cook until onions are golden, about 2 minutes. Season with salt to taste.

2 Add turmeric, chili powder, cumin, and ginger paste and cook for 2 to 3 minutes, until fragrant.

3 Using a slotted spoon, transfer shrimp to a bowl.

4 To mixture in the pan, add coconut milk powder, water, and tomato paste, stirring to combine well. Cook for 5 to 7 minutes, stirring occasionally, until thickened.

5 Return shrimp to the pan and stir gently until well coated. Cover and cook until shrimp are cooked through, about 5 minutes. Add chiles and cook for 1 more minute before serving.

· tips ·

You can use store-bought ginger paste or make your own. To make your own, simply peel ginger and then grate on a fine-toothed grater.

Coconut milk powder is available at well-stocked super-markets and Indian grocers.

Ben Kramer

Executive chef
• Diversity Food Services •
University of Winnipeg

Hometown: Regina, SK

Ben Kramer is an instigator. He wears that honour proudly as the man who continues to push the Winnipeg culinary scene in bold new directions since arriving from BC in 2000. He was an early adopter of the use of local sustainable ingredients at Dandelion Eatery, the first Ocean Wise–certified restaurant in the Prairies. Then he embarked on an ambitious project for the University of Winnipeg to completely revamp its food services program (at the time, ranked the lowest in the country among universities for food quality) while training people who fell into the hard-to-employ category. It had seemed an impossible mission until Ben appeared on the scene.

It was while running Dandelion Eatery that he was approached by the university, which was well aware that it had a major crisis on its hands. The food served to its students was terrible, and the multinational company running the kitchens didn't seem capable of turning things around. With the construction of a new residence and more students on campus, the situation could not continue.

At the same time, Seed Winnipeg, an organization offering job training for new Canadians, inner-city residents, and Aboriginal people, needed new avenues, especially in food services, to help get people working. Ben helped to put together a pie-in-the-sky business plan that would tackle both problems by tearing down the university's existing food system and rebuilding it based on the principles he valued—local, sustainable, organic—while creating new training opportunities for a new generation of food service employees.

"Basically, we took everything that is difficult and put it all into one project," he says. "I developed an idealistic plan to show how something could work in theory, without knowing whether the project would ever come to fruition."

A couple of months later, the university said it was game on and asked Ben if he wanted to head up the kitchens, backed by his supremely talented business partner Kirsten Godbout. "I jumped at the opportunity but had no idea whether what I had outlined was even possible. That was six years ago, so now I know that it really is."

The impact on the community has been profound. More than 15,000 students now have access to good food that enhances their ability to learn. And young cooks and food service staff are gaining new skills—ones that are rarely taught anywhere else, like how to butcher a whole pig.

There's a positive economic ripple effect too. The university is helping to boost the local farm economy. Running a single restaurant, Ben could buy 10 to 15 pounds of produce. Now, backed by the buying power of the university, he can commit to purchases that may be 1,500 or even 15,000 pounds. As Ben explains, "Some of the little farmers I was dealing with at the restaurant are now able to do things like build a second greenhouse because I can guarantee to buy what they can produce. It's been amazing to see everyone grow along with us."

The greatest reward for him, though, has been the forging of new young chefs—chefs who share his belief system about how things should be done and the kind of suppliers that need to be supported. "Cooks used to ask me why we were washing dirt off the vegetables when we could buy them already clean and prepped. I knew that the ingredients I was buying were better for you, better for the environment, and better for the farmers."

Nowadays, he doesn't have to explain those things: his staff get it. "I don't want to say that I've indoctrinated them, but I have. To see the belief system, drive, and passion that I've cultivated within myself for years, to see that in other people is the ultimate payoff. They make good decisions in the kitchen not because it's their job or I told them to, but because they believe it too."

> *I think it comes down to having a sense of purpose. I have an opportunity to take the gifts I've been given and to share them. If I didn't, I'd be doing a disservice to those gifts.*

37 ben kramer

One of my favourite summer activities is foraging for mushrooms. I try to take the staff out to do this a few times a year, but it is most special when it's just me and my son, Eli. This dish can be thrown together fairly quickly. With a butane burner and a bit of planning, it can be cooked on the trunk of your car or out in the woods.

soft polenta with stewed mushrooms & parsley salad

serves 4 to 6

parsley salad

3 tbsp extra-virgin olive oil

4 tsp fresh lemon juice

2 cups roughly chopped fresh flat-leaf parsley

3 shallots, thinly sliced

3 tbsp capers, roughly chopped

Coarse sea salt

1 In a small bowl, whisk together olive oil and lemon juice.

2 In a serving bowl, combine parsley, shallots, and capers. Pour oil mixture overtop and toss until well coated. Season with salt to taste. Set aside.

soft polenta

2 cups chicken stock

2 cups whipping (35%) cream

1 cup medium cornmeal

1/2 cup freshly grated Parmesan cheese

2 tbsp butter

1/4 cup chopped fresh flat-leaf parsley

1/4 cup chopped fresh basil leaves

1 In a saucepan, combine stock and cream. Bring to a boil.

2 Slowly add cornmeal, stirring constantly to avoid clumping.

3 Reduce heat to low and simmer, stirring constantly, until liquid is absorbed, about 20 minutes.

4 Add Parmesan and butter, stirring until incorporated. Remove from heat and stir in parsley and basil. Set aside, covered, keeping warm.

continued…

stewed mushrooms

4 tbsp olive oil, divided

4 tbsp butter, divided

4 lb assorted mushrooms, chopped

1 small carrot, minced

1 large yellow onion, diced

2 tsp fresh thyme leaves

Sea salt and freshly ground black pepper

4 cloves garlic, minced

1½ cups dry red wine

2 tbsp tomato paste

3 cups vegetable stock

1 cup pearl onions, halved

3 tbsp corn flour

1 In a skillet over high heat, heat 2 tbsp each oil and butter. Add mushrooms and cook, stirring often, until browned (you want to add colour but not release their liquid, so cooking over high heat is key). Transfer seared mushrooms to a plate.

2 Reduce heat to medium and add remaining 2 tbsp oil. Add carrot, onion, and thyme. Season with salt to taste. Sauté until vegetables are softened, about 10 minutes.

3 Add garlic and cook until fragrant, about 1 minute.

4 Add wine and cook, stirring to scrape up any browned bits from the bottom of the pan, until liquid is reduced by half, about 4 minutes.

5 Stir in tomato paste and stock.

6 Stir in reserved mushrooms and any juices they have released. Bring to a boil. Reduce heat and simmer until mushrooms are tender, about 20 minutes.

7 Add pearl onions and simmer until slightly softened, about 5 minutes.

8 Meanwhile, in a small saucepan, melt remaining 2 tbsp butter. Add corn flour and cook, stirring constantly, for 3 to 4 minutes, to cook out the raw taste of the flour. Add to stew and simmer, stirring occasionally, for 10 minutes, or until sauce achieves the desired consistency. Season with salt and pepper to taste.

9 To serve, place polenta in a large serving bowl. Top with sautéed mushrooms and sauce. Top with parsley salad.

*Goodness is calling
your grandparents ... and
those crispy caramelized bits
under the roasted chicken.*

Carl Heinrich

Bertrand Alépée

Chef
The Tempered Chef
Toronto, ON

Hometown: Paris, FR

Bertrand Alépée could have just written a cheque to show his support for The Stop, a Toronto-based Community Food Centre. But that would not be in keeping with the person he is. He's a doer, a man with a hands-on approach who wants to be on the front line of change.

The chef, raised in Paris, France, first learned about The Stop while at the helm of his first restaurant in Canada, Amuse-Bouche, in 2005. He had received a letter from the organization asking him to get involved. The timing was right. Bertrand wanted to do more than just run a business. He wanted to give back.

"I had never heard about The Stop before," he admits, "but I was curious. When I learned more, I was intrigued by their approach to food issues. It's not a food bank. It's more multi-faceted. It's more than just getting a bowl of warm soup. It's about getting its members involved."

He met with Nick Saul, then executive director of The Stop, who took him through the still-under-construction food centre, pointing out where the spacious modern kitchen would be, the spaces program participants would meet in to learn about nutrition and healthy eating, and what would be planted next season in the community garden. "I was so impressed with his vision. The rest is history," Bertrand says.

It would mark the start of a long and loyal friendship between the chef and The Stop. Through the years—almost a decade now—Bertrand has dedicated his talents and time to fundraising for Community Food Centres Canada in myriad ways. He was a driving force, along with chef Chris Brown (see page 68), behind Cross Town Kitchens, which brought together a dream team of top culinary talents from Toronto's best restaurants, including Perigree, Marben, C5, Torito, and, of course, Amuse-Bouche. Together they organized some of the city's most spectacular fundraising dinners, adding $150,000 to The Stop's coffers over a three-year period. Bertrand was also able to showcase his love for local ingredients as guest chef at The Stop's popular What's on the Table dinner, an annual event.

Bertrand is modest when talking about all he has contributed to The Stop and other charities involved in food security, such as FoodShare: "To me, it's just natural. It's bred in the bone. I don't really think about it. I am just someone who likes to be involved. I like to give back. Adding my voice to make us stronger is something that is very important. Besides, it's great to be able to hang out with chefs and have fun. It's a perfect recipe."

There's another aspect to his generous spirit. "When I hear the stories from the people at The Stop, it helps to put things in perspective," he says. "I'm super lucky with what I have. It's a powerful reminder to enjoy my life a bit more today." His life includes twin baby girls. Already they are showing signs that they've inherited an appreciation for good food, an appreciation which for Bertrand started early in life: when he was just four years old he told his mom, a skilled home cook, that he was going to be a chef.

> *It doesn't matter where you come from or what you do for a living; everyone deserves to have the same level of healthy food and to be able to make healthy choices.*

At age 15, Bertrand enrolled at Institut Valet in France. After graduating, he worked at Le Bistrot de l'Etoile and Le Byblos des Neigres with Alain Ducasse before moving to Canada to chef at Inn at Manitou in McKellar, Ontario—and being warmly embraced by the community of chefs in the province.

These days, Bertrand and his wife, Ruth, are looking forward to when their daughters are old enough to visit local farms. Like their father, the girls will understand the importance of good food, where it comes from, and the role it plays in everyone's life.

Most people are intimidated by cooking duck, but you don't need to be.
This is an easy and delicious way to impress your friends!

duck breast with truffle jus, roasted carrots & parsnip purée

serves 4

duck breast

1 tbsp oil

2 duck breasts (about 1 lb each)

Sea salt and freshly ground black pepper

1 Preheat the oven to 400°F.

2 In a heavy oven-proof skillet (preferably cast-iron) over medium heat, heat oil.

3 Season duck breast with salt and pepper to taste.

4 Place duck breast in the pan skin side down and cook until skin becomes nice and crispy, about 3 minutes (the duck will render a lot of fat while cooking).

5 Pour off excess fat from the pan (to ensure duck does not boil in its own fat) and transfer the pan to the preheated oven; roast for about 4 minutes.

6 Remove the pan from the oven, flip breast over, and return to the oven for another 4 to 5 minutes, until cooked through (when touched, the duck breast should feel like the meaty part of your thumb inside your palm).

7 Remove the pan from the oven and let rest on a wire rack for 2 to 3 minutes. Slice duck thinly and serve immediately, drizzled with truffle jus, with roasted carrots and parsnip purée (recipes follow).

continued…

roasted carrots

1 lb multicolour heirloom carrots, peeled and cut into long strips

4 tbsp olive oil

2 tbsp pure maple syrup

2 cloves garlic, chopped

2 sprigs fresh thyme, chopped

1 sprig fresh rosemary, leaves only, chopped

2 bay leaves

Sea salt and freshly ground black pepper

1 Preheat the oven to 350°F. Line a rimmed baking sheet with parchment paper.

2 In a large bowl, combine carrots, oil, maple syrup, garlic, thyme, rosemary, and bay leaves. Season with salt and pepper to taste.

3 Spread evenly over the prepared baking sheet.

4 Bake in the preheated oven for about 15 minutes or until carrots are nicely browned and crisp-tender.

parsnip purée

2 cups whipping (35%) cream

3 medium parsnips, peeled and cut into small chunks

2 bay leaves

1 sprig fresh rosemary

1 sprig fresh thyme

Sea salt

1 In a large saucepan, combine cream, parsnips, bay leaves, rosemary, thyme, and salt to taste. Bring to a boil, reduce heat, and simmer until parsnips are soft and falling apart, about 15 minutes.

2 Strain parsnips, reserving liquid.

3 Transfer cooked parsnips to a blender. Blend on high speed until smooth, adding just enough reserved cooking liquid to reach desired consistency. Taste and adjust seasoning.

truffle jus

½ tsp truffle oil (see Tip)
4 shallots, roughly chopped
2 cloves garlic
1 cup port
4 cups chicken or duck stock
2 sprigs fresh rosemary
2 sprigs fresh thyme
2 bay leaves
1 tsp whole black peppercorns
½ cup butter

1 In a saucepan over medium heat, heat truffle oil. Add shallots and garlic and cook, stirring occasionally, until shallots are caramelized, about 4 minutes.

2 Remove the pan from heat. Add port and return to heat. If using a gas stove, carefully tilt the pan so port ignites; if using an electric stove, hold a lit match near port to ignite it. Cook until flame extinguishes itself and liquid evaporates, about 5 minutes.

3 Add stock, rosemary, thyme, bay leaves, and peppercorns. Bring to a boil, then reduce heat and simmer for about 1 hour, until reduced by half, using a slotted spoon to skim off skin that forms on top.

4 Strain through a fine-mesh sieve into a clean saucepan (discard solids). Bring to a boil, then whisk in butter until completely incorporated. Set aside, keeping warm until ready to serve.

· tip ·

You can find truffle oil in well-stocked supermarkets or fine food stores. A little goes a long way.

4 Remove the pan from heat and add port.

5 Return to heat. If using a gas stove, carefully tilt the pan so port ignites; if using an electric stove, hold a lit match near port to ignite it. Cook until flame extinguishes itself and pears are crisp-tender, about 2 minutes.

6 Remove the pan from heat and set aside until ready to serve.

crème anglaise

5 egg yolks

6 tbsp + 1 tsp granulated sugar

1 cup whole milk

1 cup whipping (35%) cream

1 vanilla bean

1 In a bowl, whisk together egg yolks and sugar until well combined. Set aside.

2 In a saucepan, combine milk and cream. Slice vanilla bean in half lengthwise and carefully scrape seeds into the pan (save pod for another use). Bring to a boil.

3 Pour half of the milk mixture into the bowl with yolks and whisk to combine, then pour mixture into the pan.

4 Reduce heat to low and cook, stirring constantly with a wooden spoon, for about 2 minutes, until mixture thickens slightly.

5 Using a fine-mesh sieve, strain mixture into a clean bowl set on top of a larger bowl filled with ice. Let cool.

assembly

1 To assemble, place a few spoonfuls of crème anglaise in the center of each serving plate. Top with millefeuille. Arrange the caramelized pears around the millefeuille. Drizzle pear caramel over everything.

Brad Long

Chef
Cafe Belong
Toronto, ON

Hometown: Port Dover, ON

"If you don't use local ingredients first and foremost, then you're an idiot." Welcome to Brad Long's unique brand of sugar-free candour. He's a chef who tells it like it is, and that has made him a strong, vocal leader in the national food scene. He seems to have a finger in every pie.

Brad's a familiar face at fundraising and non-profit initiatives—Second Harvest, Feast of Fields, The Stop, Knives & Forks, to name a few. He sits on the Toronto Food Policy Council, and he's behind the stove at his eco-centric eatery, Cafe Belong (part of the Evergreen Brick Works). He's also well known for dishing out tough love on Food Network Canada's popular *Restaurant Makeover*.

He really has "been there and done that" over a remarkable career spanning more than 30 years. Fortunately, he's a generous sort, eager and willing to share his knowledge in hopes of educating and shaping the attitudes of new generations.

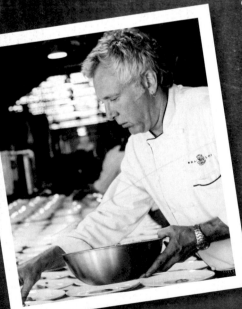

For Brad, growing up in Port Dover, Ontario, eating local was a normal part of family life. Shopping included putting some change into a jar at the end of a farmer's driveway in exchange for a basket of beautiful produce. His mom talked to her son about the importance of nutrition, proper diet, and health—and grew alfalfa sprouts and mung beans in the kitchen. "We ate good food. We ate local. We ate a variety of things. It wasn't wild or philosophical. It just made sense," he says.

In 1995, he was hired by the CN Tower to take the helm of its new restaurant, 360, and develop a menu based on Canadian cuisine. "I don't know how I got the job. I was chef of Pronto Restaurant, had done a three-month stage in Italy, and trained in classical French and

Italian cuisine at George Brown College. What did I know about Canadian cuisine? We had a few things—poutine from Quebec, butter tarts from Ontario—but regional cuisine hadn't really developed yet."

But Brad did understand that regional cuisine had to come from what was right there, a mash-up of ethnic influences and produce from farms with responsible growing practices. It's what he grew up with. Anything else was not acceptable. That became evident the day a rep from a large produce supplier came by the restaurant with the promise of great produce, all season long, trucked in from California. Brad marched him out of his kitchen and told him to never come back.

> *When you go somewhere to eat and it's really cheap, ask why. Don't ask why local food is more expensive. If you ask, then you're implying that you don't think it has value.*

Unlike some chefs, Brad sees seasonality as a gift. "It adds a factor of difficulty," he says, "but it's like having a party every month when a new ingredient is in season. Why have asparagus in November? Wait to get it in June. Then it becomes a celebration, something you crave. Just because you can have access to the same ingredients year round doesn't mean you should."

Brad is no stranger to farming. To get the right ingredients, he spends his time visiting farmers to ask questions about animal husbandry practices, paddock management, seed selection, how they treat the soil, what they spray and don't spray. "That's my job as a chef. But so few chefs do this, because they aren't trained for it." One of Brad's goals is to change that by having conversations with leading culinary programs. "It's slowly evolving," he says. "It used to be, 'Here are your ingredients. Just shut up and cook.' Now chefs are challenging the status quo."

Battling food myths and ignorance is a battle Brad is determined to fight: "I'm a soldier. Maybe more of a general by now. I'm a guy who puts his boots on the ground and is just trying to walk the talk. Food and knowledge is an absolute joy to me, and that's something I want to share with everyone."

This variation on an American classic is a favourite both in the cafe and on our family table. We always make quite a large batch because it's delicious the next morning under sunny-side-up eggs and some Neal Brothers salsa. In fact, it's hard to find something it doesn't go with.

don valley pudding

serves 8

¼ lb unsalted whey butter (see Tip)

5 cups fresh corn kernels cut off the cob (6 to 8 ears)

1 cup chopped yellow onion (1 large onion)

4 extra-large eggs

1 cup whole milk

1 cup whipping (35%) cream

½ cup yellow cornmeal

1 cup ricotta cheese

3 tbsp chopped fresh basil leaves or picked micro basil

1 tbsp liquid honey

1 tbsp kosher salt (adjust to taste)

¼ tsp chopped or puréed fresh jalapeño or serrano pepper

¾ cup shredded aged (extra-old is best) Gouda cheese (we prefer Thunder Oak or Mountainoak brand), plus more for sprinkling

1 Preheat the oven to 375°F. Lightly butter the inside of 8 individual-sized ramekins.

2 In a very large sauté pan over medium-high heat, melt butter. Add corn and onion and sauté until onion is softened, about 4 minutes. Remove from heat and let cool slightly.

3 In a large bowl, whisk together eggs, milk, and cream. Slowly whisk in cornmeal and then ricotta. Add basil, honey, salt, and jalapeño, stirring to combine.

4 Add cooked corn mixture and cheese and stir well. Divide evenly among ramekins. Sprinkle tops with additional shredded cheese.

5 Place ramekins in a large baking pan and fill the pan with hot tap water until water reaches halfway up ramekins. Bake in the preheated oven for 40 to 45 minutes, until the tops begin to brown and a knife inserted in the centre of a ramekin comes out clean. Remove from the oven, transfer ramekins to a wire rack, and let sit for a few minutes to set. Serve warm.

· tip ·

Whey butter is made from whey cream (left over from cheese-making) that's churned into butter. It has a superlative depth of flavour that's slightly nutty, earthy, and silky like a beautifully ripened soft cheese. In all fairness, any other butter will work for this recipe (but I really don't think you should be cheap nor cavalier when it comes to food, do you?).

These biscuits are a perfect accompaniment to a bowl of soup, as an edible tool to sop up jus left behind after your share of roasted chicken has somehow disappeared from your plate, or to savour the last drops of sauce that came over, on, and under that delicate piece of pan-seared fish. Me? I just slather them with butter and wolf them down while they're still warm from the oven.

leek & oatmeal biscuits

makes 8 biscuits or mini loaves

4 tbsp butter

1 cup roughly chopped leeks, white and tender green parts

$^1/_2$ cup cold whole milk

1 egg

1 cup large-flake rolled oats

$^2/_3$ cup all-purpose flour

2 tsp baking powder

1 tsp granulated sugar

1 tsp sea salt

1 Preheat the oven to 425°F. Line a baking sheet with parchment paper or butter your favourite small moulds (I use tiny bread moulds, for $2^1/_2$- × $1^1/_2$-inch loaves).

2 In a skillet over medium-low heat, melt butter. Add leeks and sauté until very tender (do not brown), 15 to 20 minutes. Remove from heat and let cool.

3 In a bowl, whisk together milk and egg. Add cooled leeks and melted butter, oats, flour, baking powder, sugar, and salt, stirring to form a thick batter.

4 Use your hands to shape batter into 8 rough rounds and place on the prepared baking sheet, or distribute batter evenly among moulds, if using.

5 Bake in the preheated oven for 10 to 15 minutes, until golden and very crisp on the outside but still extremely moist inside. Remove from the oven and let cool slightly on baking sheet. Serve warm.

Carl Heinrich

Chef
Richmond Station
Toronto, ON

Hometown: Courtenay, BC

At age 12, Carl Heinrich's mom changed his life with a new household rule. She asked each of her three kids to cook one meal a week. As a single working mom in Courtenay, BC, she needed them to help out as much as they could. Carl's go-to dish was "porcupine," a casserole with meatballs, rice, and sliced onions. He was meticulous to the point where he would keep rearranging the meatballs to get them just right.

Carl remembers now not only the dish but also the feeling that came along with it: "It made me appreciate food that tastes good. There was such a sense of pride from feeding my family and making meals the best I could." Before he had finished high school, he was cooking pretty much every meal.

His win on season two of the competitive cooking show *Top Chef Canada* ensured that Carl would be able to feed others too. He was ready after graduating from Stratford Chefs School and stints at high-profile eateries like Daniel Boulud's DB Bistro Moderne in New York.

With his $100,000 prize money, his entire life savings, and backing from a strong business partner (friend, fellow chef, and butcher Ryan Donovan, who he met a decade earlier at culinary school), Carl was able to open his very first restaurant in 2012, the 80-seat, split-level Richmond Station, located near the Toronto Eaton Centre. Word of mouth and positive reviews helped fill the restaurant. Carl's approachable comfort food, coupled with a relaxed vibe that encourages dining, not just eating, keeps it that way.

"We don't order food like other restaurants," he explains. "They might use one or two suppliers. The same company that supplies paper towel may also bring

you your week's order of mushrooms. At Richmond Station, we have somewhere in the neighbourhood of 40 to 50 producers. I have relationships with each person growing and raising that food. Our potatoes arrive with dirt still on them. I feel very strongly about the need. You can't make good food without starting with good ingredients."

That philosophy extends outside the restaurant. He's active with the Regent Park food bank and Community Food Centres Canada through his donations and cooking at awareness-boosting events. "Good food is not a luxury; it's a right," he says. "I feel that restaurants have an obligation to be a part of their communities. It's a real pleasure to go to these events that are much bigger than you are. And besides, working along other chefs is so much fun. There's such camaraderie."

What doesn't excite him is being labelled a celebrity chef. "I don't see myself that way. I was on a TV show," Carl explains. "There *are* celebrity chefs in Canada—ones that sleep four hours a night and deserve every bit of fame they get. I applaud them. For me, what I love to see is my staff, of around 50, going

Part of my job is taking care of people when they come through the door of my restaurant. That job also applies to those in my community.

further than me—like my pastry chef, Farzam Fallah, who is being recognized as a top talent in the city. My greatest joy is to see my staff running with an idea they've come up with. My attitude is 'Let's try it!'"

Carl has seen trends come and go over his career. He's not interested in following any of them except for one: "The only trend I follow is making delicious food every day. I'm excited any time I get to feed people."

5.9 *carl heinrich*

Trout Bourguignon is a Richmond Station classic. It has all the flavours of a typical bourguignon dish (red wine, onion, mushroom, and bacon), but it is broken apart and put back together with a bit of elegance. The key is the quality of the ingredients.

slow-cooked trout bourguignon

serves 4

1 cup dry red wine

2 tbsp ruby port

1 small shallot, sliced

½ cup cold unsalted butter, cut into pieces

8 sunchokes, unpeeled, scrubbed

Sea salt and freshly ground black pepper

Oil, for drizzling

2 shallots, sliced into thin rings

1 cup milk

½ cup all-purpose flour

Oil, for frying

1 cup peeled and diced rutabaga

2 tbsp butter

4 slices bacon, cut into lardons

8 small crimini mushrooms, halved

4 fillets trout, skin on (4 oz each)

4 leaves Swiss chard, chopped

Pinch finishing salt

1 In a saucepan over medium heat, combine wine, port, and sliced shallot and cook until reduced by three-quarters, about 15 minutes.

2 Pour through a fine-mesh sieve into a small saucepan (discard shallots) over medium heat. Add cold butter a piece at a time, whisking constantly until all the butter has been added and melted. Set aside, keeping warm.

3 Preheat the oven to 400°F.

4 In a roasting pan, toss together sunchokes, salt and pepper to taste, and a drizzle of oil. Bake in the preheated oven until very tender, 35 to 40 minutes. Remove from the oven and let cool. Cut in half length-wise and set aside.

5 Break shallot slices into individual rings. Place in a small bowl and cover with milk; set aside to soak for 10 minutes. Drain (discard liquid).

6 In a small bowl, toss together shallot rings and flour.

7 In a pot over medium-high heat, heat oil. Shake off excess flour from shallot rings and shallow-fry (in batches if needed so as not to crowd the pan) until lightly golden brown, about 1 minute. Transfer fried shallots to a plate lined in paper towel. Season with salt and pepper to taste.

continued…

8 In a large saucepan, cover rutabaga with water and bring to a boil. Boil until very tender, about 30 minutes. Drain well.

9 Transfer cooked rutabaga to a blender and add 2 tbsp butter. Blend on high speed until puréed. Season with salt and pepper to taste.

10 In a clean skillet over medium-high heat, cook bacon until fat has rendered and bacon is lightly caramelized, about 5 minutes. Transfer bacon to a plate lined in paper towel, reserving fat in the pan.

11 To same skillet, add mushrooms; cook for about 5 minutes, stirring occasionally, until lightly caramelized. Drain oil and set mushrooms aside to cool.

12 Reduce the oven temperature to 250°F. Line a baking sheet with parchment paper.

13 Season trout on all sides with salt and pepper to taste. Place skin side up on the prepared baking sheet. Bake in the preheated oven for 7 to 10 minutes, until you can just peel skin away from the flesh.

14 In a skillet over medium-high heat, heat 1 tbsp oil. Add roasted sunchokes and sauté until golden brown, about 5 minutes. Add cooked bacon, cooked mushrooms, and Swiss chard; cook, tossing in the pan, until Swiss chard is wilted, about 1 minute.

15 Spoon rutabaga purée onto a serving platter. Top with sunchoke mixture. Pull skin off trout and discard. Season trout with finishing salt, then place on top of vegetables and drizzle with reserved red wine sauce. Top with shallot rings and serve immediately.

**Goodness is
better than beauty.**

Vietnamese proverb

This dish is a great example of how to use all of a local ingredient. At Richmond Station, we only buy whole animals, directly from the farmer, and only from southern Ontario. We know all our producers well, and this helps us find the best-quality ingredients out there.

caramelized onion perogies *with* braised beef shank & celery root purée

serves 4

braised beef

2 tbsp oil

1 lb beef shank

4 cups beef stock

1 cup dry red wine

1 sprig fresh rosemary

1 sprig fresh thyme

1 small bay leaf

1 Preheat the oven to 250°F.

2 In a large skillet over medium-high heat, heat oil. Add beef shank and sear on all sides until well caramelized, about 5 minutes per side. Add stock and wine and bring to a simmer. Add rosemary, thyme, and bay leaf; cover and braise in the preheated oven until meat is fall-off-the-bone tender, about 3 hours.

3 Transfer braised shanks to a plate and cover to keep warm. Place the pan with liquid over high heat and skim to remove all of the fat on top. Reduce until thick, about 30 minutes. Cut braised meat into small pieces and add to reduced liquid. Cover and set aside, keeping warm.

continued…

perogy filling

3 russet potatoes, unpeeled

2 tbsp vegetable oil

2 onions, thinly sliced

3 green onions, thinly sliced

¼ cup sour cream

8 oz aged cheddar cheese, shredded

Sea salt and freshly ground black pepper

1 Increase the oven temperature to 400°F. Stab the potatoes with the tines of a fork and place directly on the middle rack in the oven. Bake until very soft, about 1 hour. Set aside to cool slightly.

2 Slice cooled potatoes in half and, using a spoon, scoop out flesh and place in a bowl (discard skins). Pass potatoes through a ricer, or mash with a masher.

3 Meanwhile, in a skillet over medium heat, heat oil. Add onions and cook until caramelized, about 5 minutes. Reduce heat to low and continue to cook until very soft, about 20 minutes.

4 Add caramelized onions, green onions, sour cream, and shredded cheese to potatoes. Season with salt and pepper to taste and stir to combine. Set aside.

perogy dough & assembly

½ cup sour cream

6 tbsp melted butter

1 large egg

1 large egg yolk

2 cups all-purpose flour, plus more for dusting

1 In a bowl, stir together sour cream, melted butter, egg, and egg yolk. Fold flour into wet ingredients. Turn out onto a slightly floured work surface and knead until a smooth and slightly elastic dough forms.

2 On a lightly floured work surface, roll out dough to 1/8-inch thickness. Using a glass, cut out as many rounds as you can. Place about 2 tbsp of filling on half of each round. Fold dough over filling to make a half-moon shape and pinch edges to seal. (You may need to brush with a small amount of water to help the dough stick together.)

3 Bring a large pot of salted water to a boil. Prepare an ice bath.

4 Add perogies to boiling water and boil for 3 minutes. Using a slotted spoon, transfer perogies to the prepared ice bath. Once cool, transfer perogies to paper towels to drain.

celery root purée

1 small celery root, cut into small
pieces (reserve yellow leaves)

2 tbsp butter

¼ cup sour cream

1 Place celery root in a saucepan and cover with water. Bring to a boil and cook until very tender, about 30 minutes. Drain.

2 Transfer to a blender, add butter, and blend on high speed until smooth. Scrape purée into a bowl and fold in sour cream. Set aside.

assembly

3 tbsp butter, divided

1 small head celery,
peeled and diced

1 In a skillet over medium-high heat, melt 2 tbsp butter. Working in batches if needed (so as not to crowd the pan), fry boiled perogies until crisp on one side, about 4 minutes.

2 Meanwhile, in a saucepan of boiling water, blanch celery until just crisp-tender, about 1 minute. Drain in a colander and transfer to a bowl. Add 1 tbsp butter and toss until well coated.

3 To serve, spread celery root purée evenly over a serving platter. Top with fried perogies and then braised beef. Scatter blanched celery overtop and garnish with reserved celery root leaves. Serve immediately.

Chris Brown

Owner & chef
• Citizen Catering •
Toronto, ON

Hometown: Unionville, ON

If Chris Brown had a motto, it might be "We're all in this together." When it comes to building communities, he has been an ardent supporter, whether it's through his time as chef at The Stop Community Food Centre in Toronto or by bringing together the city's top chefs to fundraise. He just thinks that way. He understands that the power of one is amplified when surrounded by like-minded people.

One of those people is fellow chef Bertrand Alépée (see page 42). The two got to know each other at Montreal's Lumière festival. As Chris explains, "We went to do this amazing event where Toronto chefs were paired with other restaurants. It was an incredible collaboration between two cities. Afterward, Bert and I ran into each other on the street in Montreal. We were kind of in awe over the event. We wondered, 'Why isn't this happening in Toronto? Why aren't we collaborating? We are neighbours—we should be working together, not competing against each other.'"

That was the beginning of an all-star group of five Toronto chefs called Cross Town Kitchens, and creating a community of people who cared about good food and making a difference. It started holding fundraiser dinners for The Stop and, within its first year, was able to donate $80,000. In the process, Chris got to know The Stop's former executive director Nick Saul, so when Nick called to say he wanted to chat, Chris accepted the invite.

Nick was well aware of the success of Cross Town Kitchens. Chris recalls the meeting: "He asked, 'Why don't you make me some money?' I thought about it.

I had just closed my restaurant Perigree. I was in limbo. I was miserable. So I started working at The Stop. I was so thrilled because I had all these ideas, like introducing a catering business."

When Nick gave him a tour of the facility, Chris saw the dining room filled with community-meal-program participants. He felt like it was a perfect fit for him. "This is my 2 percent," he says, referring to a social experiment he did while a culinary student at George Brown College. When people on the street asked him for money, he asked them if they'd like to have a meal instead. Chris took those who said yes out for a meal and paid for it. That happened in just 2 percent of the cases. He wondered how he could connect to those people on a broader, meaningful scale. It was clear his answer was through The Stop.

"My job is to feed people whether they have money or not," he says. "And I love feeding people and making them happy through food." He had an opportunity to do that at The Stop for five years before he bought its catering company and set out on his own as Citizen Catering. "My time at The Stop was really rewarding. Nick was a great mentor, and I loved working with him to help find solutions for hunger and poverty."

It's not just a question of feeding people. It's about education, showing people the difference between good and bad food.

Chris still gets to do what he enjoys most: nurturing people through good food, and supporting The Stop and other non-profits that do the kind of work that matters most to him. He continues to demonstrate his generosity of spirit by creating events like Chefs for Change, an event that brought together 30 chefs from across the country for a series of fundraising dinners, with net profits going to Community Food Centres Canada. Giving is just part of who he is.

"I'm a firm believer in community. If a community works together, it's able to solve problems a lot quicker and empower people to overcome problems. And if you can help, why not?"

6.9   *chris brown*

This recipe is from my wife's great-uncle Jack, who is one of the most interesting men I know. I am lucky enough to spend many of my summer weekends at the cottage with him, snacking on these pickles over a grilled burger while playing a couple rounds of liar's dice.

bread & butter pickles

makes about six 1-litre jars

30 cucumbers, sliced crosswise

12 onions, sliced

½ cup pickling salt

5 cups granulated sugar

4 cups white vinegar

2 tbsp mustard seeds

2 tbsp celery seeds

2 tbsp ground ginger

1 tbsp ground turmeric

1 In a large non-reactive bowl, combine cucumbers and onions. Add salt and toss to combine. Let sit for 30 minutes.

2 Meanwhile, in a large pot, combine sugar, vinegar, mustard seeds, celery seeds, ginger, and turmeric. Bring to a boil, then reduce heat and simmer for 15 minutes.

3 Drain cucumbers and onions well under cool running water; rinse and drain well again. Gently pack into sterilized jars (see Tips).

4 Carefully pour pickling liquid into jars, leaving a ½-inch headspace. Using a butter knife, remove any air bubbles in jar, readjusting headspace if necessary by adding more cucumbers and pickling liquid. Cover with the prepared lids (see Tips) and screw on until fingertip tight.

5 Boil in a boiling water canner for 15 minutes (see Tips). Store in a cool, dry place until ready to use. Will keep for up to 1 year.

· tips ·

To sterilize jars, place jars upright on a wire rack in a large pot. Cover the jars with hot water (make sure jars are completely submerged), cover pot, and boil for 10 minutes. Prepare the lids according to the manufacturer's instructions.

When processing jars, make sure the jars are covered by at least 1 inch of water. Bring to a rolling boil before starting processing time.

Blanching stinging nettles removes the stinger-like fine hairs these plants are known for so you can enjoy their woodsy flavour (just be sure to wear gloves when handling them raw). Pairing them up with wild mushrooms takes this forest-inspired dish to the next level.

wild mushroom & stinging nettle gnocchi

serves 4

1 large russet potato

5 oz wild stinging nettles

8 oz ricotta cheese

3 egg yolks

1 cup all-purpose flour, plus more for dusting

1³/₄ oz freshly grated Parmesan cheese

1 tbsp melted butter

2 tsp kosher salt

9 oz mixed wild mushrooms, sliced

4 tbsp olive oil, divided

3 pinches kosher salt

Freshly ground black pepper

½ cup water

1 tbsp unsalted butter

Asiago cheese, for grating

1 Preheat the oven to 400°F.

2 With the tines of a fork, poke each potato three times. Place on a baking sheet and bake in the preheated oven until tender, about 45 minutes.

3 Meanwhile, bring a large pot of heavily salted water to a boil. Prepare an ice bath.

4 Carefully add nettles to boiling water (be sure to wear gloves) and blanch for 15 seconds. Using a slotted spoon, immediately transfer to the prepared ice bath to cool.

5 When cool enough to handle, roughly chop. Set aside.

6 Using a ricer or food mill, pass cooked potatoes into a bowl. Add ricotta, egg yolks, flour, Parmesan, melted butter, and salt. Stir until a soft dough forms.

7 Bring a large, covered pot of water to a rapid boil.

8 Divide dough into 4 equal parts. Lightly dust a clean work surface. Using your hands, gently roll dough into long cylinders about ½ inch in diameter. Using a sharp knife, cut cylinders into mini gnocchi each about ½ inch long. Gently press the tines of a fork into each gnocchi to make slight indentations. Dust lightly with flour.

continued…

9 Place gnocchi in boiling water and cook until they float to the top, about 1 minute. Using a slotted spoon, transfer gnocchi to a large tray.

10 Preheat the oven to 400°F.

11 In a bowl, toss mushrooms with 2 tbsp oil and pinches of salt and pepper. Spread on a roasting pan and roast in the preheated oven for 10 minutes.

12 To finish, in a large skillet, bring 1/2 cup water to a boil. Add remaining 2 tbsp oil and butter, stirring until butter is melted. Add cooked gnocchi, nettles, and mushrooms, tossing to combine. Heat through, 1 to 2 minutes. Transfer to a large platter and grate Asiago overtop. Serve immediately.

*Goodness is seeing kids,
the next generation, make
great food choices.*

Ryan Donovan

Elana Rosenfeld

Co-founder & CEO
· Kicking Horse Coffee ·
Invermere, BC

Hometown: Toronto, ON

The beaches of Thailand aren't typically a place you'd create a detailed business plan for starting a coffee company, but that's where the seeds were first sown for Kicking Horse Coffee. Elana Rosenfeld and her partner, Leo Johnson, sat on the sand with pen and paper plotting out their future company. "We started from a very humble place," she says, laughing.

Even before they knew what their venture would be called, they had already named the blends of coffee they would sell out of Invermere, a small town (population not quite 4,000) not far from Kootenay National Park in eastern BC but far from everything else. It seemed like an impossible dream, and prompted Elana's mom to ask, "What are you two schmucks going to do? Sell coffee out of your garage?" That's precisely how it all started.

It's almost two decades later and Kicking Horse Coffee has become Canada's number one organic and fair trade coffee brand. It employs more than 85 people, and last year roasted somewhere in the neighbourhood of 3.5 million pounds of coffee. Those are perfect conditions for Elana to do what she finds the most gratifying: create and nurture communities.

As a fair trade certified coffee, Kicking Horse helps communities worldwide by ensuring growers receive an equitable market price for their beans. "I've seen first-hand the positive impact of this," says Elana. "In just five

elana rosenfeld

> # Giving back is deeply ingrained in who I am. I like to do the right thing. I love the opportunities we can help create for other people.

years, the infrastructure of a community becomes stronger because of it." It's just part of "doing the right thing," a phrase she uses often in explaining the choices she makes.

After a woman in Invermere told Elana about fair-trade practices, long before they were in the public consciousness, she knew immediately that this was the way to go, despite the naysayers who said she'd never be able to find a supply. In explaining her decision to go organic, she says: "I have a vegetable garden and I wouldn't use pesticides on it. So I wouldn't do that with coffee I sell. I want everyone drinking good coffee, whether they care about organic or fair trade or not. It's a bonus if they do. It helps to open a discussion about it."

Originally from Toronto, Elana fell in love with the mountains, and her adopted hometown has been good to her. She feels that her success is a direct result of the support she's had there: "The sense of community is all around you," she says. "We shop at the same stores, our kids go to school with those of our employees ... We're all connected."

The very long list of charities, events, and local initiatives Kicking Horse Coffee is involved in touches on everything from the arts (the Banff Mountain Film and Book Festival) to the environmental (Nature Conservancy of Canada) to sports (Trek Dirt Series—Mountain Bike Camp). Elana can't help but be involved. "I don't do things halfway," she says. "I love people who do good things, and I love to support that. I love to see people be successful." That also applies to the new businesses sprouting up in town, businesses that have caught on to Kicking Horse Coffee's can-do attitude. Elana couldn't be more thrilled. "What you give, you receive," she says.

elana rosenfeld

These little angels have all kinds of angles. Locals say they taste like "another." Many have tried but failed to eat only one. For a soft little number, these scones are a big hit in the Kicking Horse Café. Incidentally, they pair extraordinarily well with a favourite cuppa something warm.

rocky mountain scones

makes 16 scones

4 cups all-purpose flour

1 cup granulated sugar

3 tbsp baking powder

1 tsp sea salt

1 cup cold unsalted butter

1¼ cups whipping (35%) cream

4 large eggs

3 cups berries of your choice (blueberries, raspberries, hulled and halved strawberries)

1 Preheat the oven to 350°F. Line a baking sheet with parchment paper.

2 In a bowl, combine flour, sugar, baking powder, and salt.

3 Using two knives, a pastry cutter, or your fingers, cut in cold butter until mixture resembles small peas.

4 In another bowl, whisk together cream and eggs. Add to flour mixture along with fruit and gently stir until just combined (be careful not to over-stir; dough should be dry but not crumbly).

5 Turn dough out onto a clean work surface and lightly flour. Divide into 2 equal portions.

6 Shape each portion into a flat circle about ¾ inch thick. Cut each circle into 8 triangles.

7 Transfer to the prepared baking sheet and bake in the preheated oven for 15 to 17 minutes, until lightly browned and a tester inserted into the centre of a scone comes out clean.

8 Let cool on pan for 30 minutes before serving.

Free spirits, free minds, free thinkers, and even free radicals can all agree on one thing: these cookies are a chain reaction of goodness. Ain't no gluten in these discs of deliciousness, but they've got all the ingredients for a big bite of juicy *Mmmmm-hmmmm*. Perhaps there should be a food group called "cookie"? You be the judge.

kicking horse café's gluten-free cookies

makes 6 dozen cookies

9 cups gluten-free flour

3 ¾ cups puffed rice cereal

3 ¾ cups dried unsweetened cranberries

3 cups granulated sugar

3 cups semisweet chocolate chips

3 cups raw sunflower seeds

2 ¼ cups raw pumpkin seeds

¾ cup flaxseeds

3 tbsp ground cinnamon

2 tbsp + ¾ tsp sea salt

3 cups almond milk

2 ¼ cups canola oil

½ cup molasses

1 Preheat the oven to 350°F. Line a baking sheet with parchment paper.

2 In a large bowl, combine flour, cereal, cranberries, sugar, chocolate chips, sunflower seeds, pumpkin seeds, flaxseeds, cinnamon, and salt.

3 In another bowl, combine milk, oil, and molasses. Add wet ingredients to dry ingredients and stir until just combined.

4 Using a small ice-cream scoop, scoop batter onto the prepared baking sheet, leaving about 1 inch between each mound. Using your fingers or the back of the scoop, press down on each mound to flatten slightly.

5 Bake in the preheated oven for 5 minutes. Rotate the baking sheet and bake until slightly browned, about 8 more minutes. Remove from the oven and let cool on the baking sheet for 5 minutes before transferring to a wire rack to cool completely.

· *tip* ·

This recipe can be halved, but why not make the whole batch and share them with friends?

Unlike a push-up, the French press is a simple exercise:
brew a coffee full of goodness. Life's too short to drink the wrong
cup of coffee, so here's the 411 on getting it right, every time.

kick ass
french-press coffee

makes 1 cup

3 tbsp coarsely ground coffee

1 cup filtered water

1 Place ground coffee in the French press.

2 Boil water, then let sit for 30 seconds.

3 Pour hot water into the French press, stirring gently.

4 Allow coffee to "bloom" to within 1 inch of the rim.

5 Let steep for 4 minutes.

6 Stir once, plunge gently, and pour into a coffee cup.

7 Enjoy! (Inevitably, there will be sediment at the bottom of your cup; discard it.)

· tips ·

To ensure the coffee is fresh, check the "enjoy by" date on the package. Or squeeze a little air from the package: it should smell deep, dark, and delicious.

For best results, grind whole beans just before brewing.

Use fresh, cold, filtered water. Great water makes good coffee taste great.

Say no to the refrigerator or freezer. Instead, store coffee beans in a dark, cool, dry place, in the original packaging or an airtight container.

Kick Ass® is a registered trademark of Kicking Horse Coffee.

Goodness: food, friends, fun in equal measure, and quality, carefully curated, never forgotten. That is goodness to me!

Steve Cooper

Gillian Flies

Grower
• The New Farm •
Creemore, ON

Hometown: Williamstown, VT

After leaving her family's farm in Vermont and moving to Toronto, Gillian Flies had no intention of returning to farm life. It's funny how things change. Now she and her husband, Brent Preston, are like rock stars, lauded by chefs, retailers, and fellow farmers for showing that you can be successful while staying true to your beliefs as an organic grower.

It started in 2003 when they bought a rundown 100-acre farm near Creemore, Ontario. They originally intended it to be a weekend getaway, and a way to provide their family with more opportunities to grow better food—the kind Gillian grew up with.

Gillian fondly remembers coming home from school to churn butter from the fresh milk her father brought in from their cows, and the dinner-table stories about where the food in front of them came from and who had made it. She wanted to bring that kind of good food back to the dinner table so that her son and daughter could have the same experiences.

"I was amazed," she recalls. "I couldn't find organic produce." So she slipped on her rubber boots and overalls and returned to the soil to grow food for her family. Then she began selling some of her vegetables at the Creemore farmers' market, and then eventually to restaurants. The demand went through the roof. These days, produce from The New Farm supplies 50 restaurants and a dozen retail stores.

That could have been a tidy success story of its own, but Gillian and Brent had something bigger in mind. "It wasn't in our DNA to grow these beautiful, healthy vegetables just for the affluent," Gillian explains. "We wanted everyone to have access." The couple started a CSA (community-supported agriculture) program in which customers could buy a basket of food for themselves and also purchase one to donate to The Stop, a Toronto Community Food Centre offering drop-in meals, education, and food bank services.

"Then we realized that what we could send to The Stop was a drop in the bucket toward feeding its 16,000 clients," she says. Fundraising kicked into high gear with The New Farm's annual food and music event, attracting 700 guests, big-name chefs, sponsors such as Neal Brothers Foods, and performers like Sam Roberts and The Tragically Hip. They also launched a retail brand called Grow for The Stop, where 10% of the purchase price is donated to The Stop to buy organic produce from other small local farmers. To date, The New Farm has donated more than a quarter of a million dollars to The Stop, all of which has been used to buy local, organic vegetables.

"We certainly didn't get into organic farming to get rich. We have kids of our own, and we can see the difference healthy food can make. We have come at this from a human-rights and compassion angle," Gillian emphasizes. That's a driving force for her and Brent in their quest to increase the number of organic farmers by taking on apprentices, offering farm tours, working with new growers, and boosting education through public speaking.

The payoffs of Gillian's activism touch every part of her family's life. She can watch her kids eat raw broccoli and strawberries straight out of the field, knowing that they are free of harmful pesticides and herbicides. She's proud to watch former apprentices flourish with their own organic farms. Her biggest source of pride is serving as a model for others, showing that you can be both an organic grower and successful.

"It's the hardest job we have ever had," says Gillian, "but it's so rewarding to be part of something so positive for the world."

I still have to explain why organic and sustainability matter. People need to understand that they are charging the cost for cheap food to the environment. To stop that, we need to pay the real cost for it.

8.5 *gillian flies*

This dish is a crowd-pleaser. For a more rustic dish, use organic carrots and scrub the skin rather than peel it off; this will also allow the maple syrup and butter to coat the surface better.

maple-glazed carrots

serves 4

8 medium to large carrots (preferably multicolour)

2 tbsp butter

½ cup pure maple syrup

1 Slice carrots lengthwise.

2 Fill a saucepan with 1 or 2 inches of water. Place a steamer insert inside and fill with carrots. Cover and steam carrots over medium heat for about 8 minutes, just under crisp-tender (make sure carrots do not become too soft, as they will continue to cook in step 4).

3 In a skillet over medium heat, melt butter. Add maple syrup and heat until small bubbles appear.

4 Add steamed carrots and gently stir to coat well. Cook until syrup and butter mixture has boiled up around carrots and candied them, 2 to 5 minutes. Serve immediately.

Beet greens are delicious and incredibly good for you. This recipe was a favourite of my children when they were young. The tamari reduces the bitterness of the greens and allows the sweet flavour to come through.

sautéed beet greens

serves 4

2 tbsp olive or canola oil

1 tbsp sesame oil

2 cloves garlic, chopped

1 large bunch beet greens (see Tip), trimmed and finely chopped

2 tbsp tamari or teriyaki sauce

1 In a saucepan over medium-high heat, heat oils. Add garlic and sauté until fragrant, about 1 minute.

2 Add greens and stir until well coated, about 1 minute.

3 Add tamari and gently stir to combine. Sauté until greens have wilted slightly, 3 to 5 minutes.

4 To serve, place cooked greens in a serving dish and drizzle sauce overtop.

· *tip* ·

You can substitute kale or chard leaves for the beet leaves.

This dish is a regular at our farm. I like to use multicoloured beets because we grow them on the farm, and because they look beautiful, but you can use any colour you like. The maple syrup and heat cause the beets to candy and become sweet and delicious. Cold leftover beets are fabulous served on a salad the next day.

roasted beets

6 to 8 medium beets, trimmed and scrubbed

3 tbsp pure maple syrup

2 tbsp balsamic vinegar

2 tbsp chopped fresh parsley or French tarragon leaves

2 tbsp olive oil

Sea salt and freshly ground black pepper

1 In a large saucepan, cover beets with water and bring to a boil. Boil for 30 to 40 minutes, until tender.

2 Transfer beets to a bowl or sink full of cold water. Using your fingers (wear gloves, if desired, to prevent staining your hands), slip skins off beets (discard skins).

3 Using a sharp knife, cut beets into 1$\frac{1}{2}$-inch cubes.

4 Place beets in a bowl. Add maple syrup, vinegar, and parsley. Let sit for 1 to 2 minutes to marinate.

5 Preheat the oven to 400°F. Grease a glass baking dish with oil.

6 Pour beet mixture into the prepared baking dish and roast for 20 to 45 minutes, until beets are candied and tender (they will have reduced in size by about one-third).

7 Remove from the oven and season with salt and pepper to taste. Serve.

Ian Walker

President
Left Coast Naturals
Vancouver, BC

Hometown: Niagara-on-the-Lake, ON

Ian Walker is a man on a mission. He's out to change the world and to leave it a better place. That might sound ambitious to some people, but he's making it happen by adopting policies around sustainability, organic, and non-GMO foods unlike any others. His approach is about doing good by being good— embodying what it means to be a responsible, ethical business.

And he's succeeding on all fronts. Left Coast Naturals, his manufacturing and distribution company that sells certified organic food across 30 brands and 200 bulk items, will become the first company of its type in North America to ban genetically modified organisms (GMOs) along its entire supply chain, from farmer to distribution partners, by the end of 2015.

That's not the only thing that earns bragging rights. Left Coast Naturals also donates a minimum of 5 percent of its profits to charity and gives its staff three paid days off a year to do volunteer work in the community. And the cherry on top is that Ian spends a good chunk of his time inspiring others to do the right thing through education programs and mentorship of like-minded companies.

Though Left Coast Natural rings in revenue around $20 million, that's not the stick by which Ian measures success. "What's important to me is having a business I am proud of, as well as my kids and future grandkids," he says. "If I don't accomplish that, I haven't accomplished anything."

Ian is a guy that is as nice as they come, but there's a hint of rebel to his personality. He will zig while others zag, and he's not afraid to be the lone voice in a crowd when it comes to ringing alarms bells around food ethics. Yes, he and some of his colleagues really did attend an industry event wearing "F*CK GMOs" T-shirts. It's part of his mandate to push and to question.

Even as young bucks fresh out of university, a quest for sustainability—based on the three Ps—people, planet, and prosperity—shaped the decisions Ian and his friend Olympic athlete Jason Dorland made as they started a business selling their homemade organic nut butters at Vancouver's Granville Island Market in 1996. It wasn't meant to be the beginning of a career in food, but it turned out that way when the orders from retailers flooded in. "Right when we started, we were a mission-aligned business," he says. "It had to fit with who we were as people. I knew enough about business that we knew we wanted to be different, and that has resonated over the years."

There's no doubt that Ian has led his business down a different path. He's hardcore about ensuring that the products he sells are as natural as nature intended and goes to great lengths to ensure they are using third-party validation, external audits, and internal score cards for growers and suppliers, who look at everything from soil usage to water management.

> ## Money isn't the reward or the end goal. It's about doing something good.

If the results are not in keeping with company values, Ian is prepared to walk away from orders totalling hundreds of thousands of dollars. He shrugs it off, saying, "I am okay with making less when it means achieving our mission. Because success to me is having a business that is perfectly aligned with who you are as a person." It's that conviction that makes him a popular speaker at events on sustainability and food safety. He's someone who really does walk the talk as a good corporate citizen.

Oddly, sharing the company's remarkable story wasn't something that happened until recently. Left Coast Naturals did not even have a marketing department until about four years ago. Ian was persuaded to enter the limelight because he recognized it was an important way to inspire others. "It's just not my thing," he admits. "I am a reluctant leader that way. I would rather focus my energy on doing the right things."

93 *ian walker*

My grandparents had a cottage on Lake Temagami in Northern Ontario, and every summer my siblings and I would visit them. I have fond memories of my grandmother making this cake from the blueberries that grew on their property (in fact, she wouldn't make this cake using any other blueberries!). We carry on that tradition with our own kids, using grandma's recipe and the berries that still grow on the land.

blueberry buckle cake

makes one 9- × 12-inch cake

2 cups all-purpose flour

2 tbsp baking powder

½ tbsp sea salt

¾ cup granulated sugar

½ cup butter, softened

1 large egg, beaten in milk, to measure 1 cup

1 tsp pure vanilla extract

1½ cups fresh blueberries

4 tbsp all-purpose flour

4 tbsp butter

¾ cup granulated sugar

1 tsp ground cinnamon

1 Preheat the oven to 350°F. Lightly grease a 9- × 12-inch baking pan.

2 In a bowl, sift together 2 cups flour, baking powder, and salt.

3 Using an electric mixer on medium speed, cream together ¾ cup sugar and ½ cup butter. Add egg and milk mixture and vanilla, and mix until combined.

4 Slowly mix in dry ingredients just until combined. Fold in blueberries. Pour batter into the prepared baking pan. Set aside.

5 In another bowl, combine 4 tbsp flour, 4 tbsp butter, ¾ cup sugar, and cinnamon. Sprinkle streusel topping evenly over batter.

6 Bake in the preheated oven for 35 minutes, or until a tester inserted into the centre of the cake comes out clean. Let cool in pan slightly before serving.

This cake is inspired by a recipe by the fantastic chef Richard Sax. The "hippie flakes" is my twist. I prefer to make this using all organic ingredients.

chocolate cake with hippie flakes

makes one 8-inch cake

8 oz semisweet chocolate, coarsely chopped

½ cup unsalted butter, cut into pieces

2 large eggs

4 large eggs, separated

1 cup granulated sugar, divided

¼ cup strong brewed coffee (we prefer fair trade)

1½ cups whipping (35%) cream

1 package (56 g) coconut chips (we prefer Hippie Foods brand), smashed into small pieces (see Tip)

· tip ·

To smash coconut chips to make Hippie Flakes, place on a clean kitchen towel, fold over towel, and roll over with rolling pin.

1 Preheat the oven to 350°F. Line the bottom of an 8-inch springform pan with parchment paper (no need to butter the pan or the paper).

2 In a bowl, using a double boiler or microwave, melt chocolate (microwave chocolate on High for 15-second increments until melted).

3 Whisk in butter until melted and well combined. Set aside.

4 In another bowl, whisk together whole eggs, egg yolks, and ½ cup sugar just until combined. Slowly whisk in melted chocolate mixture. Whisk in coffee.

5 Using an electric mixer on medium speed, beat egg whites until foamy. Slowly add remaining ½ cup sugar and beat until soft peaks form. Gently fold beaten egg whites into chocolate mixture. Pour batter into the prepared pan and, using a rubber spatula, smooth top.

6 Bake in the preheated oven for 35 to 40 minutes, until puffed up and cracked and no longer jiggly in the centre (be careful not to overbake).

7 Remove from the oven and let cool completely in the pan on a wire rack. (Don't worry: the cake will fall as it cools and make a sort of crater in the centre. That's for the whipped cream.)

8 To unmould cake, run the tip of a knife around cake edge and then carefully remove the side of the pan.

9 When ready to serve, whip cream. Fill cake crater with whipped cream. Top with coconut flakes.

Jamie Kennedy

Chef
Toronto, ON

Hometown: Don Mills, ON

If ever there were to be a designated poster boy in Canada for growing and using locally sourced ingredients, it would be Jamie Kennedy. The Order of Canada recipient continues to inspire his peers and a younger generation of chefs. He leads change by doing, by setting an example. No soapbox needed. He understands that what he does as one of Canada's top chefs gets noticed. So he's the guy happy to lend star appeal to charity events, ensuring surplus food gets to food banks and community meal programs, or connecting in a real way to people who produce the food he serves.

Jamie vividly remembers a moment when he was 10 years old that would set the scene for his career as a chef: he took a bite of a simple salad made with fresh tomatoes his dad had bought at a farm stand near their home in Don Mills, a suburb of Toronto. "Wow! Does this ever taste good!" he thought. It was a full sensory experience that would be the impetus for getting involved in the local-food movement.

Working as an apprentice at a fine-dining restaurant in a luxury Toronto hotel, he was often disappointed with the food there: "Very rarely did it come from a local market. I always felt at odds with the level of quality of those ingredients because I had memories of that salad and of wild blueberries from where my aunt lived south of North Bay, and of fresh peaches.

"I thought it was such an irony. This was fine dining, yet we didn't have access to better ingredients. At the time, I was very young and thought there must be some reason behind that. But then I started to really champion the idea of good-tasting food, not just fancy food. That was my inspiration to get involved in the local-food movement." At the time, he was a lonely locavore (before that term even existed). He didn't have connections to the people producing the ingredients he used. "I knew there had to be a better way to be more connected. I found it locally within my community," he says. Fast-forward 40 years and many restaurants later, and his passion for good food is burning as bright as ever.

It's not just the quality of ingredients that Jamie has pushed into the spotlight. It's also the ideas of how they impact communities and finding ways to make farming sustainable. "The model of the small family farm in Ontario disappeared a century ago," he explains. "What took its place is not really environmentally sustainable. People are now more invested in producing food for future generations. There are solutions. They're out there."

Local food tastes better. And there is something about local procurement that lends more satisfaction to the whole exercise, whether I'm cooking for my family or for guests at my restaurant.

One of those solutions is what he calls the "value-added prospect." Rather than local growers trying to compete with growers of tomatoes, say, in Mexico or California, they can turn their tomatoes into something else, like salsa or sauce. By doing that, they create a value-added prospect, which is local and commands a much higher price.

"Being a bit more entrepreneurial is definitely the order of the day," Jamie says. "Gone are the marketing boards that protect specific growers of certain things. There's not a lot of quality associated with that. Quality is where the new economies will define themselves."

The chef is getting his hands dirty, working the soil himself to produce food. A few years ago, spurred on by his love of growing grapes and making wine, he bought a 100-acre farm in Prince Edward County. Now he's growing vegetables for his restaurant, taking produce from his fields to his tables. But he says that his time behind the stove is coming to an end: he has decided to sell his restaurant and get out of the business so he can devote himself to growing food for others. Once again, he is leading and inspiring by example.

jamie kennedy

Back in 1998, when I had my restaurant at the Royal Ontario Museum,
I made the switch from serving farmed Atlantic salmon to serving wild Pacific.
I had prepared the farmed salmon for a group of First Nations guests from BC.
One by one they politely refused it. They did not support farming salmon and
inspired me to find out more about it. This dish makes a wonderful first
course. Serve it with blanched asparagus and a small salad.

marinated wild sockeye salmon

serves 6

2 cups sea salt

2 cups granulated sugar

1 bunch fresh dill, roughly chopped

Coarsely ground black peppercorns

1 fillet wild sockeye salmon, skin on (about 1½ lb)

2 bunches fresh dill, roughly chopped

Coarsely ground black peppercorns

1 In a bowl, combine salt, sugar, first measure of dill, and pepper to taste.

2 Sprinkle an even layer of cure on the bottom of a non-reactive container that is long and deep enough to comfortably fit fillet. Lay fillet on top, skin-side down. Liberally sprinkle fillet with cure. Sprinkle remaining cure around the edges of fillet. Cover and refrigerate for about 8 hours.

3 Rinse fillet under cold running water. Pat dry with paper towel and place in a clean non-reactive container. Set aside.

4 In a bowl, combine second measure of dill and pepper to taste; stir to form a paste. Press an even layer onto flesh side of cured fillet. Cover and refrigerate for 6 hours before serving.

This recipe has become a family classic. It is hard to say for sure where rösti originated. The Swiss would fiercely defend it as their own. So would the Austrians. In any case, I'm glad for whoever invented it, as it inspired me to make bacon and eggs in a new and exciting way. This rösti looks great on the plate and is fun to serve the whole family as a late breakfast on the weekend.

bacon rösti *with*
cheesy scrambled eggs

serves 4

bacon rösti

10 oz unsliced smoked bacon, cut into lardons

4 large russet or Yukon Gold potatoes, peeled and grated

1 medium onion, finely diced

Sea salt

4 tbsp butter, divided

1 In a skillet over medium heat, sauté bacon until crisp, 5 to 7 minutes. Set aside.

2 Place grated potatoes in the middle of a clean kitchen towel. Bring ends of towel together and twist to squeeze out excess liquid from potatoes. Transfer to a non-reactive bowl.

3 Add cooked bacon and onion. Season with salt to taste. Stir to combine. Divide into 4 equal portions.

4 In a nonstick pan over medium heat, melt 1 tbsp butter. Using your hands, form one portion of potato mixture into a pancake and place in the pan. Slowly fry until golden brown on each side, about 3 minutes per side. Transfer to a baking sheet and place in a warm oven. Repeat with remaining butter and potato portions.

continued…

cheesy scrambled eggs

8 large eggs

7 tbsp butter

2 medium onions, finely diced

½ cup finely grated 2-year-old cheddar cheese

2 tbsp finely chopped fresh chives

2 tbsp milk

1 In a non-reactive bowl, whisk together eggs. Set aside.

2 In a large saucepan over medium-low heat, melt butter. Add onions and gently sauté, taking care not to brown onions at all. Add beaten eggs and cook, stirring constantly, until eggs are set. (I like to take my time with this step as the consistency of the eggs is best when cooked slowly. This will take about 10 minutes.) Remove from heat and stir in cheese and chives. While stirring constantly, add milk.

3 To serve, place a rösti on each of 4 warmed serving plates. Mound cheesy scrambled eggs on top. Serve immediately.

*The roots of all goodness
lie in the soil of appreciation
for goodness.*

Dalai Lama

Jean-François Archambault

CEO & founder
· La Tablée des Chefs ·
Montreal, QC

Hometown: Ste-Rose, QC

When Jean-François Archambault studied hotel management at Institut de tourisme et d'hôtellerie du Québec (ITHQ), he had a chance to spend some time in the kitchen cooking. In the process of practising and being graded, he and his classmates would cook four times what they were able to eat. The leftover food was dumped into the garbage. That wastefulness upset Jean-François, and he vowed to do something about it.

Jean-François had a vision for a food-recovery program in which unwanted food would be taken from hotels and caterers and given to shelters and food banks. It was a simple yet innovative idea. But getting started was challenging. People feared the potential liability issues involved with food safety. But, Jean-François says, "I was not going to accept 'no' for an answer."

His determination was fuelled by memories. When he was nine years old, he and his brother and sister collected used toys for low-income families at Christmastime. "We didn't understand why anyone would want something used," he remembers. "Then my dad took us to meet a poor family with three children who didn't live far from us. When they saw us with the used toys, they were so happy. Seeing something like this marks your life."

The final push came when his mother died at age 49. "It was like a kick in the butt," he says. Despite being previously told no by hotel managers and chefs, he was determined to find a way to start his food-recovery program,

La Tablée. He cleared the legal hurdle with help from his dad, a lawyer, who discovered a Good Samaritan act—a civil law that removed the worries of reprisal—thus opening the door to food donations.

Jean-François solicited support from young chefs attending culinary schools who were open to new ideas. Then the Bell Centre agreed to try the food-recovery service. It had been throwing out more than half a ton of food left over in its executive suites after each Montreal Canadiens game. Hotels began to follow suit and enlisted the services of La Tablée. The program took off.

Once there was some income, La Tablée could afford to hire a coordinator. Jean-François quit a comfortable job as regional director for sales and marketing and took on the position, which paid two-thirds less. He has no regrets. "I explained to my wife that it's like having a baby and being faced with giving it up for adoption. I couldn't stand that," he says. "I know exactly what I want to do with this, and I am the one who should be doing it."

Jean-François recognized that addressing hunger was just one piece of a much bigger, complex puzzle. In response, he launched a culinary camp for youth ages 12 to 17—one that had them learning about nutrition and cooking alongside famous chefs and Montreal Canadiens hockey players. The camp was a success, and before long the program had been introduced into 4 high schools in underprivileged neighbourhoods. Now it's in 60 schools across Quebec, with hopes of hitting the 200 mark in five years.

As for the food-recovery program, it now recovers 500,000 meals a year in Montreal and has been rolled out in Toronto, Ottawa, Calgary, and Mexico City. There is also a cooking program for youth coming out of foster care, plus two cooking schools for the general public. But that's not enough. As Jean-François points out, "This is just the beginning."

> *My strength is putting the pieces together. Chefs? They have food. And the shelters and food banks need food. Why not connect them to help feed communities?*

107 *jean-françois archambault*

I love to start with ripe avocado and get creative with fresh herbs and any other ingredients I have on hand. I serve this guacamole with tacos, but it's also great with grilled fish such as cod or mahi mahi.

zesty guacamole

makes about 3 cups

2 ripe avocados, pitted and peeled

3 ½ oz cream cheese

3 ½ oz labneh (see Tip)

⅓ cup olive oil

1 cup fresh basil leaves

½ tbsp champagne vinegar

Zest and juice of 1 lime

1 clove garlic, minced

1 In a large bowl, roughly mash avocado with a fork. Add cream cheese, labneh, olive oil, basil, vinegar, lime zest and juice, and garlic.

2 Using a hand mixer on low speed, slowly crush the mixture until you reach desired texture (either smooth or chunky works—whatever you prefer!).

3 Transfer to a serving bowl and enjoy.

tip

Labneh is a lightly salty soft cheese made from yogurt. It is available in well-stocked supermarkets or Middle Eastern grocers. If you can't find any, you can substitute an equal amount of thick sour cream or even cream cheese.

This dish is a great way to use up leftover salmon, especially if you barbecued a full fillet for the whole family. Leave it on the counter for your guests to nibble on as they keep you company in the kitchen. Serve with Homemade Croutons (recipe follows).

salmon rillettes

serves 6 as an appetizer

2 tbsp capers, drained

10 oz cooked salmon

3 ½ oz cream cheese

3 ½ oz English cucumber, finely diced (about ⅔ cup)

1 small shallot, minced

Zest and juice of ½ lemon

3 tbsp finely chopped fresh dill

2 tbsp finely chopped fresh cilantro

2 tbsp extra-virgin olive oil

Sea salt and freshly ground black pepper

1 Crush capers using a mortar and pestle. Transfer to a mixing bowl.

2 Add salmon, cream cheese, cucumber, shallot, lemon zest and juice, dill, cilantro, oil, and salt and pepper to taste. Mash with a fork until you achieve a spreadable consistency.

3 Transfer to a serving bowl. Place on a wooden cutting board and surround with homemade croutons.

homemade croutons

Serve these tasty croutons with salmon rillettes. They are also wonderful with a cheese course and soup.

1 day-old baguette, cut into ½-inch-thick slices

extra-virgin olive oil, for drizzling

Sea salt

1 bunch fresh rosemary, leaves finely chopped

1 Preheat the broiler to High. Line a baking sheet with parchment paper.

2 Arrange baguette slices in a single layer on the prepared baking sheet.

3 Drizzle oil in a zig-zag motion over the baguette slices. Sprinkle with salt to taste. Sprinkle with rosemary.

4 Place on top oven rack and broil for 7 to 10 minutes, until toasted and golden brown (keep a close watch so they don't burn). Remove from oven and cool slightly before serving.

Jenn Prager

Family support worker
Dartmouth Family Centre
Dartmouth North Community Food Centre
Dartmouth, NS

Hometown: Dartmouth, NS

There's no mincing words when it comes to how Jenn Prager feels about the Dartmouth Family Centre: "It changed my life; it changed who I am; it changed the opportunities that my kids will have in their futures."

She was introduced to the organization in 2006 when, as a mom with three kids all under the age of four, she wanted to get out of the house with her young family and meet new people. She enrolled in Jump, Jiggle, and Jive, a parent–child interactive program. Right off the bat, she recognized it was a special place for her and other members of her community. But she wanted to do more than take classes. She signed on as a volunteer in 2009, then later jumped at a chance to join the staff, working part time three days a week in fall 2014.

To say it has been rewarding doesn't describe her experience accurately. Working at the centre has ignited a passion in her about issues like food security, supporting local farmers, and the importance of providing adequate social assistance to those in lower-income households. The Community Food Centre arm of the family centre is launching in October 2015 in a newly renovated space, and Jenn is also excited to see more nutrition and cooking programs being offered to the community, from seed planting to a class for young cooks. Like other Community Food Centres across Canada, the Dartmouth North Community Food Centre is bringing people together to grow, cook, share, and advocate for good food for all.

"It empowers the community by providing people with somewhere to gather, somewhere they won't be judged, somewhere they feel welcome, whether it's to sit and have a cup of coffee or to take a class. It's part of owning the space and building relationships. Once those supports between people are made, the community strengthens."

If there is anything that gets Jenn riled up, it's hearing the stereotypes and myths that still permeate society about people who use food programs. "I've seen people wait two hours for a bread truck to arrive, just to get a single loaf of bread," she says. "I hear people tell me that they've gone to multiple food banks trying to get enough food to feed their families. That's not lazy."

Her passions for social justice and good food are now shared by her children. Her oldest son also does volunteer work, and the entire family picks up a CSA (community-supported agriculture) basket each week and goes regularly to local farms to buy pork, chicken, and beef. "I love that I get to hug my farmers on a regular basis!" she says. "I try to stick to local and give money directly to the producer. I want my food vote to count for something. If more people are able to do that, good food will become more easily accessible for everyone."

These days, her focus is also on the people she meets at the Community Food Centre. Her reward is seeing them gain confidence in themselves—like the woman who told Jenn she was far too shy to ever participate in any programs. Recently, that same woman took her aside after a cooking class and said, "Thank you for gently pushing me. I had so much fun. I can't wait to sign up for next month. I'm so glad you didn't give up on me." That's the stuff that gets Jenn excited—the changes, the new relationships, the joy of discovery. It's why she wakes up in the morning excited to get to work and face a new day.

> *I learn as much from the participants of the centre as they do from me. We're all in this together. Everyone is doing the best they can. My job reminds me of that every day.*

jenn prager

I've been making this recipe for my family for years, using either leftover turkey or leftover chicken. My youngest daughter has recently shown a huge interest in cooking, and it has been lots of fun following her instructions in the kitchen while making this chowder.

turkey chowder

serves 8

4 tbsp butter

4 carrots, diced

2 small onions, diced

2 ribs celery, diced

4 tbsp all-purpose flour

6 cups stock (chicken, turkey, or vegetable)

4 cups chopped cooked turkey

2 potatoes, peeled and diced

1½ cups corn kernels (fresh or frozen)

1 tsp dried thyme or 8 fresh thyme sprigs or 1⅓ tbsp chopped fresh thyme

Sea salt and freshly ground black pepper

1 In a soup pot over medium heat, melt butter. Stir in carrots, onions, and celery, coating well, and cook for 1 minute.

2 Remove the pot from heat and stir in flour. Reduce heat to low, return the pan to heat, and cook vegetables for 1 minute.

3 Add stock and bring to a boil. Add turkey, potatoes, corn, and thyme and cook for 15 minutes, or until potato is tender. Season with salt and pepper to taste.

Any version of mac & cheese is well received in my household, but this homemade version is by far my family's favourite. My kids help grate the cheese and make bread crumbs from the ends of bread loaves (that no one eats otherwise!).

macaroni & cheese

serves 4 to 6

3 tbsp butter

3 tbsp all-purpose flour

2 cups milk

3 to 4 cups shredded cheese of your choice, divided

Sea salt and freshly ground black pepper

2 to 3 cups dried macaroni pasta

1 to 2 cups diced cooked ham

½ to 1 cup dry bread crumbs

1 Bring a large pot of salted water to a boil.

2 Meanwhile, in a saucepan over medium heat, melt butter. Stir in flour (to create a roux) and cook for 1 minute. Add milk and bring just to a simmer. Add 2 cups cheese and cook, stirring constantly, until cheese is melted and sauce thickens, 2 to 3 minutes. Season with salt and pepper to taste.

3 Add pasta to the pot of boiling water and cook until al dente, according to package instructions. Drain well.

4 Preheat the oven to 350°F.

5 Transfer cooked pasta to a lightly greased casserole dish and stir in ham.

6 Pour sauce evenly over top; stir until pasta is well coated. Sprinkle with remaining 1 to 2 cups shredded cheese, then bread crumbs.

7 Bake in the preheated oven until cheese topping is melted and bread crumbs are browned, about 30 minutes. Let sit for 5 minutes before serving.

John Lai

Chef in training
Prince Edward County, ON

Hometown: Wellington, ON

When John Lai initially volunteered at The Stop Community Food Centre in Toronto, he had no idea what to expect from the experience. All he knew was that he was interested in food and cooking, so it seemed like a good fit. As he became more familiar with the depth and range of The Stop's programs and facilities, from community gardens to food bank services and nutrition classes to its state-of-the-art greenhouse, he got hooked. He spent more than six years working onsite, doing food prep, helping to make breakfast, before he became a chef's assistant and helped to cook meals for up to 200 people. He had found his calling.

"At first, I have to say, I didn't really know what The Stop did," John explains. "But when I learned more, I was so inspired by their work. I really enjoyed the time I spent there. When I volunteered, it was with the idea of wanting to do something bigger than myself, something for the greater good."

He found himself evolving from volunteer to food activist. "People need education. They need skills for the long run. Having access to good food is a valuable insurance program. If you eat well, you're less likely to get sick. It's so important for people to put good food in their bodies and to understand nutrition."

John's own education through The Stop sparked him to make a life-changing decision. When he was laid off from his job as a graphic designer, he needed a plan B. This gave him a chance to start a second career in the profession he loves. John enrolled in the George Brown College culinary program, graduating in October 2014. He has a fire in his belly to spread the word about good food and healthy eating.

Good food should be a part of everyone's health insurance program, along with education and kitchen skills that are useful in the long run.

Fresh out of school, he landed a job at Drake Devonshire, a chic boutique hotel in Prince Edward County. Although John is not in Toronto and volunteering at The Stop anymore, he has taken what he has learned with him. He's in the beginning stages of starting a program in conjunction with a registered dietitian in which he teaches financially challenged families to cook nutritious healthy meals using a typical hamper provided by the local food bank.

He credits his Chinese background for helping him form his food-as-medicine beliefs. "Growing up, my siblings and I encountered a lot of food on the table that tasted kind of medicinal, such as ginseng chicken soup," he recalls. "We were told that it was good for us, so we ate it. We learned that food can have that role. It's not just about sustenance. It's about taking care of your health."

John also points to Nick Saul, who became executive director of The Stop in 1998, as someone who helped fuel his desire to volunteer and make a difference. "Annual general meetings are not normally very exciting, but every AGM for The Stop that I attended left me feeling completely energized. Nick is a charismatic leader. He has such a clear vision of what he wants to accomplish."

John will never forget what he witnessed after one particular AGM whose guests included a slew of chefs and VIPs. When the last guest had left, Nick picked up a broom and swept the floor. "I think about his leadership when I want to do something out of my comfort zone. He has no idea how much he inspires me, or how much money he saved me by not having to go to Tony Robbins seminars. Nick is truly a hero figure to me."

john lai

This soup is a variation of a traditional dish called *bak kut te*, which literally translates to "meat bone tea." In Singapore, the Chinese enjoy this soup for breakfast. This variation uses seasonings easily found in a bulk-food store.

side ribs soup

serves 4 as an appetizer or 2 as a main course

8 cups water

¼ cup soy sauce

2 tsp sea salt

2 whole star anise

3 2-inch cinnamon sticks

1½ tbsp goji berries

1 lb pork side ribs, cut into riblets

1 In a large pot, bring water, soy sauce, salt, star anise, cinnamon sticks, and goji berries to a boil (this will be the soup's base).

2 Add ribs and bring to a boil. As soon as soup comes to a boil, reduce heat and simmer, covered, for 40 minutes, until meat is tender (thickest part of meat should reach 165°F on a cooking thermometer).

3 Divide ribs among soup bowls. Ladle over soup base. Serve with rice (see Tip) or whole-grain bread for dipping.

tip

Traditionally a bowl of steamed rice is served alongside the soup. When eating the soup, you spoon broth into the rice bowl to flavour the rice. You then take a bite of the rib meat and a spoonful of flavoured rice, and chew on the delicious combination.

This tasty chicken curry is popular in Malaysia and Singapore.
Every family has their own variation of the spice mix; this is mine.
Serve with steamed rice or lightly toasted naan.

malaysian chicken curry

serves 4

1½ tbsp curry powder

1 tbsp chili flakes

1 tsp ground turmeric

1 tsp ground cumin

¼ cup vegetable oil

½ medium red onion, diced

2 fresh red chile peppers, sliced open and seeds intact

5 thin slices peeled fresh gingerroot

2 cloves garlic, sliced

½ cup tomato paste

4 medium potatoes, unpeeled, quartered

2 lb chicken, cut into 8 pieces

3 cups water

2 whole cardamom pods

2 whole star anise

2 whole cloves

1 3-inch cinnamon stick

1⅔ cups coconut milk

2 tsp sea salt or to taste

1 In a small bowl, combine curry powder, chili flakes, turmeric, and cumin. Stir in just enough water to make a paste. Set aside.

2 In a large saucepan over high heat, heat oil until it shimmers. Reduce heat to medium and add onion, chile peppers, ginger, and garlic and cook, stirring constantly, for 2 minutes, until fragrant (be careful not to burn them). Add prepared spice paste and cook, stirring, for 2 minutes, until well combined and flavours meld. Stir in tomato paste.

3 Increase heat to high. Add potatoes and stir to coat potatoes in spices. Cook for about 10 minutes. Add chicken and stir well to coat. Add water, cardamom, star anise, cloves, and cinnamon, and bring to a boil. Reduce heat and simmer for 10 minutes.

4 Stir in coconut milk and simmer for 20 minutes, until potatoes are tender and chicken is cooked through (see Tip). Add salt.

5 Discard whole spices before serving. Serve immediately.

· tip ·

In step 4, if chicken is cooked through but potatoes need a little more time to cook, transfer chicken to a plate and set aside, then continue to cook the potatoes until tender. Return chicken to the pan and heat through before serving.

Joshna Maharaj

Chef
Toronto, ON

Hometown: Brampton, ON

In a rural village in India, Joshna Maharaj witnessed first-hand how food shapes lives. While at an ashram, she took a job in the kitchen and quickly fell in love with cooking. "I remember the times when the chef was in a bad mood," she says. "I could see how that would migrate into the food. You could see that mood spread across the dining hall and really affect people. I realized then the great impact chefs have. I saw the huge responsibility and opportunities a cook has. I loved the idea that I could have a positive impact on people with one pot of food."

Ever since returning to Canada and graduating from the culinary arts program at George Brown College, Joshna has been infusing everything she does with a generous helping of positivity, including the work she did at The Stop Community Food Centre and her current mission of changing the way institutions like schools and hospitals feed people. She understands that food can do more than "fill the tank." It can also nurture good health.

After her first job at Dish, Toronto's popular cooking studio, she landed at The Stop when then executive director Nick Saul asked her to help him interview to fill the position of chef. But no candidate quite fit the bill. Some had solid food management experience but lacked the understanding of the bigger socio-political implications of the work being done there. Then Nick realized that the perfect person for the position was right in front of him.

Joshna calls her time at The Stop a "very important, life-shaping experience." She came to learn that a sustainable food system cannot exist just for the people who can afford it, and that access to both good-quality food and a truly sustainable food system is a basic human right. "I was very happy to be part of a team that pushed that message," she says.

It was also hugely rewarding for her to perform miracles routinely with the limited food and the tiny, tiny budget that was available to her and a team of dedicated volunteers to cook lunch twice a week for 200 people. (The meal program has significantly expanded since.) Joshna was instrumental in elevating the standard of food to that of any other professional kitchen in the city. It remains the proudest accomplishment of the five years she spent at The Stop.

For her next move, she set her sights on shaking up professional kitchens. She wasn't interested in working at a restaurant—she knew there were opportunities outside that realm. In 2011, she took a job at Scarborough Hospital, with the mandate of doing an extreme meal makeover, thanks to a hospital administrator who believed in the idea and some funds to back it. "There was a huge disconnect between the nutritional advice patients were getting from the doctor and the food they were being served while in the hospital's care," she explains. "We weren't tapped into the importance of such a connection. The food was empty, mediocre, and poor quality. You have to wonder what messages were being given to patients."

Joshna set out to bridge the gap by asking hard questions and pushing for smarter solutions. By the time she left the position, patients, before taking their first bites of a beet salad, say, would read the note on their tray telling them about the farmer who grew those beets. It was Joshna's way to put the human connection back into the food system.

She worked her magic at Toronto's Hospital for Sick Children, then Ryerson University, her current employer. She's revolutionized the way these kinds of large organizations feed people by offering better, more delicious

Our idea of what chefs do has to broaden. I want to push the idea that they have a responsibility to step up and be more engaged champions of food.

and nutritious food. It's no wonder she is now a popular speaker at conferences, sharing her success stories. "I didn't start out with this idea," she says, "but I have become the institution-food lady in this town, and I couldn't be happier about it."

joshna maharaj

This is an easy and reliable recipe, with a killer cheese sauce that you can use for a variety of dishes, including mac & cheese. Adding the kale really fortifies the dish, and is how I like to serve it to students.

cauliflower kale gratin

serves 4 to 6

3 lb cauliflower (1 large head), cut into 1½- to 2-inch florets

½ bunch kale, stems removed and leaves sliced into ½-inch ribbons

¼ cup unsalted butter, divided

2 tbsp all-purpose flour

1½ cups whole milk

6 oz sharp cheddar cheese, coarsely shredded (about 2 cups)

½ cup finely chopped green onions, green part only

½ tsp sea salt

½ tsp freshly ground black pepper

20 square (2-inch) saltine crackers

1 Preheat the oven to 450°F. Butter a 2-quart shallow baking dish.

2 In a large saucepan of boiling salted water, cook cauliflower until just tender, 6 to 8 minutes. Just before the last 2 minutes of cooking, add kale and stir well. Using a colander, drain cauliflower and kale and transfer to the prepared baking dish.

3 Meanwhile, in a heavy-bottomed saucepan over medium-low heat, melt 2 tbsp butter. Whisk in flour (to create a roux); cook roux, whisking constantly, for 3 minutes. While whisking, add milk in a slow stream; bring to a boil, whisking frequently. Reduce heat and simmer, whisking occasionally, for about 8 minutes, until thickened.

4 Remove milk mixture from heat and add cheese, green onions, salt, and pepper, whisking until cheese is melted. Pour cheese sauce over cooked vegetables and stir gently to combine. Set aside.

5 Coarsely crumble crackers into a bowl.

6 In a small saucepan, melt remaining 2 tbsp butter. Pour over crumbs and toss to coat.

7 Sprinkle crumb topping evenly over vegetables. Bake in the preheated oven until topping is golden brown, about 10 minutes. Serve and enjoy.

This recipe is versatile and can make great use of leftovers like roast chicken. Quinoa is a superfood but often not cooked well. Draining quinoa thoroughly, then drying it out, will ensure a delicious light, granular finish. Swap out flavourings as you like, but make sure there's something crunchy and sweet involved.

quinoa chicken salad

serves 4 to 6

1 cup quinoa, rinsed and drained

3 pieces roast chicken (use leftovers or freshly roasted)

2 green onions, finely sliced

1 small handful seedless red grapes, halved

2/3 cup crisp, sweet apple, cored and cut into small dice

1/2 cup mayonnaise

Juice of 1/2 lemon

1/2 tsp kosher salt

1/4 tsp freshly ground black pepper

1 small handful fresh flat-leaf parsley leaves, finely chopped

1 Bring a small pot of salted water to a boil. Add quinoa and boil for 8 to 10 minutes, or until grain has plumped up and the little tails are peeking out. Drain in a fine-mesh sieve, then run sieve under cold running water to stop cooking (you should feel no warm spots when you put your hand under the sieve). Rest sieve on edge of the pot and let quinoa drain for 10 minutes.

2 Line a baking sheet with paper towel. Spread drained cooked quinoa evenly over paper towel and let dry for 30 minutes.

3 Meanwhile, pull chicken meat from bones, roughly chop, and place in a large bowl. Add green onions, grapes, and apple and stir to combine.

4 In a small bowl, whisk together mayonnaise and lemon juice until smooth.

5 Add drained quinoa to chicken mixture and toss gently to combine. Pour dressing over quinoa and season with salt and pepper. Add parsley and toss well to combine. Taste and adjust seasoning, if needed.

Judy Dempsey

Community chef
The Table Community Food Centre
Perth, ON

Hometown: Ottawa, ON

As the owner of a successful restaurant, The Hungry Planet, in Perth, Ontario, Judy Dempsey won over diners and critics alike for her fresh season-driven cuisine. There were accolades aplenty, but after a decade, she started to crave something with more meaning. "I had all the recognition and awards I could ever want," she says. "I felt satisfied with this type of work, but it wasn't quite enough." Around the same time, she was appalled upon seeing the horrible food the local high school was serving to her kids. "It was revolting. That's where I thought I could make a difference."

Making a difference and shaking things up are common threads running through Judy's life. She's always charted her own course, whether it was having a restaurant with an open kitchen before that was a thing or selling uncommon foods like rhubarb juice and spring rolls at the local farmers' market in the early 1990s when she moved to Perth from Toronto (where she had worked as a caterer for film productions). After she closed the restaurant and was no longer working 80-hour weeks, she had a chance to ponder what should come next.

As someone plugged into her community virtually since the day she arrived, Judy had heard rumblings about the local food bank. People were asking questions about its future: "What if we bought a building, changed the whole model, and turned it into a Community Food Centre?" She supported the idea and actively campaigned for Perth to be chosen as the site for one of two pilot Community Food Centres being developed in Ontario. The Table launched in 2011, and in the fall, Judy was hired to lead the kitchen and food programs.

"It was the perfect fit for me," the self-taught chef explains. "I have three passions in my life: my horse, music—specifically, Bruce Springsteen—and good food. But not necessarily in that order. I love to cook. I love to cook with people. I love to eat other people's food. I love to think about food. To be able to do what I do at The Table is an incredible gift."

She also has the chance to awaken taste buds with new tastes and ingredients, especially any related to Southeast Asian and Thai cooking. Although she's known for her love of bold flavours, she treads more lightly when serving the community meals at the Community Food Centre—but just a tiny bit. Participants know better than to ask for something to be left off their plates: they know that Judy expects them to try a little of everything, then judge.

> *Success to me is when people are happy and the dining room is alive with people eating, talking, and laughing. This place is as much about community as it is about food.*

"There are incredible rewards in just hearing people say things like 'I really feel good after I eat here' or 'I didn't think I'd ever eat kale. Now, I actually like it!'" Even her non-traditional takes on classics—for example, lasagna made with root vegetables—have won over palates. That's definitely a win, and one that supports Judy's decision to join The Table.

"I love coming to work every single day," Judy says. "I just love this job. I work with incredible people. The other staff here are passionate about what they do and really feel that the work we are doing is important. They're professional and a blast to work with. We laugh all the time. It's just a really great thing to be doing in my life."

131

judy dempsey

This soup boasts hearty flavours and is the perfect autumn comfort food. I like to use whatever winter squash is available from our local farmers or at The Table Community Garden.

chickpea & pancetta soup

serves 4 to 6

½ lb pancetta, chopped

1 large onion, chopped

1 tbsp chopped garlic

1 tsp chopped fresh rosemary leaves

4 fresh sage leaves, chopped

1 cup chopped cooked winter squash

6 to 8 cups canned chickpeas, drained (liquid reserved) and rinsed

2 cups diced tomatoes, with juice

Extra-virgin olive oil

Freshly grated Parmigiano-Reggiano cheese

Chopped fresh flat-leaf parsley leaves

Freshly ground black pepper

1 In a large soup pot over medium heat, sauté pancetta.

2 Add onion and garlic and cook, stirring often, until softened, 4 to 6 minutes. Stir in rosemary, sage, squash, and half of the chickpeas.

3 Using a food processor, purée remaining chickpeas.

4 To the soup pot, add chickpea purée and tomatoes and stir to combine. Add reserved chickpea liquid and enough water to reach desired consistency. Bring to a boil, stirring frequently. Taste and adjust seasonings.

5 Divide soup among serving bowls and garnish with olive oil, cheese, and parsley. Sprinkle with pepper and serve.

This savoury, easy Thai-influenced noodle dish is satisfying on all levels—sour, salty, spicy, and sweet. Make it year round but especially in August when juicy tomatoes, local garlic, cilantro, and green onions are in season. This is the number one request of my adult children when they return home for a visit.

spicy pork noodles

serves 2

1 tbsp vegetable oil

1 to 2 tbsp minced garlic

4 oz ground pork

1 handful dried rice noodles (about ⅓ package), soaked in warm water until slightly softened, drained

2 tbsp white vinegar or to taste

1 tbsp fish sauce or to taste

1 tbsp soy sauce or to taste

1 tbsp hot water

1 to 2 tbsp granulated sugar (to taste)

2 cups coarsely chopped tomatoes, with juice

2 fresh double kaffir lime leaves, very finely chopped

Chopped fresh cilantro leaves

Chopped green onion

Chili flakes

1 In a wok over medium heat, heat oil. Add garlic and fry until golden, about 2 minutes.

2 Add pork and cook, stirring, until it browns, 7 to 10 minutes.

3 Push pork to one side of the wok. To the other side of the wok, add prepared rice noodles.

4 Add vinegar, fish sauce, soy sauce, water, and sugar. Cook, stirring, adding hot water as required to prevent sticking, until noodles are softened.

5 Add tomatoes and cook, stirring, until noodles are tender, 3 to 5 minutes.

6 Add lime leaves, cilantro, and green onion to taste and stir to combine. Add chili flakes to taste. Serve immediately.

Judy Servay

Founder & general manager
Robin des Bois
Montreal, QC

Hometown: Montreal, QC

Helping others is a thread that has run through Judy Servay's life for a very long time. She has volunteered to feed the homeless and has worked to better lives through a youth centre. That was in addition to running a company that produced music videos. After 10 years she became bored and sold it. "What next?" she wondered. The answer came with Robin des Bois ("Robin Hood"), a restaurant where her love of business and contributing to her community could converge under one roof.

Judy isn't the type of person to follow well-worn paths. She creates her own. With Robin des Bois, she turned the typical restaurant business model on its ear. Her restaurant would be more than a place to eat; it would be a gathering place designed to bring people together to learn, to connect, and to generate funds for charity. It would largely be staffed by volunteers, from the kitchen to the dining room, and serve dishes made with locally sourced ingredients. And all profits would go directly to fund the work of four organizations working in urban Montreal to stave off poverty and social isolation.

Judy wanted to create opportunities where people could volunteer in a fun way, and a restaurant seemed to tick a lot of boxes. "Food brings together people in every country," she says. "Everyone needs to eat, and that was a main element in starting this project. Then the challenge was how to do it." Despite never having worked in a restaurant, she forged ahead, backed with advice from many good people with experience.

Right out of the gate, Robin des Bois generated a lot of buzz among diners and the media alike. Tables and bellies were kept full, and within two years, the restaurant had outgrown its location. A bigger space was in order, so it moved one block north to a location front and centre on Boulevard Saint-Laurent, one of Montreal's hippest stretches, and now seats 120.

In its new digs, the restaurant has been able to offer more, from culinary day camps for kids ages 10 to 13 to what Judy calls "a release room"—a place where, for a small donation, you can smash a plate against a concrete wall and get rid of any pent-up anger or angst—not a feature conventionally offered by restaurants, but then again, one would never think of sticking a conventional label on Robin des Bois.

First-time visitors are surprised by what they find. Many think that the charitable component of the restaurant means they'll get a mushy bowl of spaghetti in a cafeteria-style setting. Imagine the shock—and relief—when they are presented with choices such as venison steak, duck confit, and its very popular Indian-style lentil soup, against a backdrop that resembles a chic brasserie.

Judy loves to share stories about the many volunteers who come through the restaurant, from the loyal regulars and tourists to new Canadians to corporate groups embarking on team building. She talks of couples meeting there and falling in love, of people with depression volunteering to be servers and finding the strength to move forward with confidence, of families working together, then leaving with happy memories. It is those people who fuel her passion as a restaurateur.

"I love having a job that is in harmony with my beliefs," she says. "That is at the core of all this. I get to work with amazing people. It's never boring. I am always happy to walk in the door, ready to work. How many people can say that? I am very blessed."

> *It's not about the money. It's about being part of something bigger. We try to be a bit of everything to everyone.*

judy servay

Dahl is a traditional Indian soup made with lentils and a blend of spices. This version, drizzled with lime and paprika oils, is a favourite at our restaurant and has been a mainstay on our menu for the last eight years! It's easy to make, economical, and extremely nourishing.

serves 6 to 8

2 tbsp vegetable oil

2 large onions, finely chopped

2 cloves garlic, minced

1½ cups dried red lentils

1 tbsp coarse salt

1 tbsp cumin seeds

½ tsp chili flakes

6½ cups water

1 tbsp fresh gingerroot, peeled and minced

Sour cream

Lime Oil (recipe follows)

Paprika Oil (recipe follows)

Fresh cilantro leaves, for garnish

1 In a pot over medium heat, heat oil. Add onion and sauté until translucent, about 3 minutes. Stir in garlic and cook for 2 more minutes, until fragrant.

2 Add lentils, salt, cumin seeds, and chili flakes. Stir in water and continue to cook for about 10 minutes, stirring occasionally.

3 Remove soup from heat and stir in ginger.

4 Ladle into serving bowls, top with sour cream, lime oil, and paprika oil, to taste, and garnish with a few cilantro leaves. Serve.

continued…

paprika oil

2 cups sunflower or canola oil

¼ cup sweet paprika

1 tbsp sea salt

3 cloves garlic, minced

1 In a skillet over medium heat, heat oil. Add paprika, salt, and garlic and stir well. Remove from heat and let cool for 30 minutes.

2 Strain through a fine-mesh sieve into a resealable jar (discard solids).

lime oil

1 cup sunflower oil

Zest of 3 limes

1 In a resealable jar, combine oil and lime zest. Set aside in a cool, dark place for 1 week, shaking jar occasionally.

2 Strain through a fine-mesh sieve into a clean resealable jar (discard solids).

· tip ·

These recipes will make more oil than you will need for this dish. Cover and refrigerate for up to 2 weeks.

Goodness: delectable, delicious, but good for you too—all the time, never a day without goodness!

Dufflet Rosenberg

Mujaddara is a hearty lentil stew from North Africa traditionally served over rice. While the berbere spice mix contains a long list of ingredients, it is worth making (it also goes well with braised beef or lamb) and will keep for up to a year in an airtight container.

mujaddara

serves 4

2 tbsp oil

1 large onion, cut into ½-inch dice

1 large carrot, cut into ½-inch dice

2 stalks celery, cut into ½-inch dice

2 cloves garlic, minced

1½ cups dried black Beluga lentils (see Tip)

3 tbsp tomato paste

4 to 5 fresh thyme sprigs

1 bay leaf

2 tbsp Berbere Spice Mix (recipe follows)

4 cups vegetable stock

Fresh cilantro leaves, for garnish

Fried onions, for garnish

Steamed rice, for serving (optional)

1 In a large pot, heat oil. Add onion, carrot, and celery and sauté until softened, about 5 minutes. Add garlic and cook until fragrant, about 2 minutes.

2 Stir in lentils, tomato paste, thyme, bay leaf, and berbere. Pour in stock and bring to a boil. Reduce heat and simmer for about 30 minutes, stirring often, until lentils are tender.

3 Divide steamed rice (if using) among serving bowls. Ladle lentils overtop and garnish with a few cilantro leaves and fried onions. Serve.

tip

If you can't find Beluga lentils, you can substitute green lentils—just keep an eye on them, as they will require a shorter cooking time.

continued…

berbere spice mix

¼ cup Armenian pepper

¼ cup Korean pepper flakes
or piment d'esplette

¼ cup sweet paprika

2 tbsp ground coriander

2 tbsp ground ginger

2 tsp ground green cardamom

2 tsp onion powder

2 tsp sea salt

2 tsp freshly ground black
peppercorns

2 tsp fenugreek, toasted and
ground (see Tips)

2 tsp freshly grated nutmeg

1 tsp ground cinnamon

1 tsp garlic powder

1 tsp ground black cardamom

1 tsp ajwain or dried thyme

½ tsp ground cloves

1 In a resealable jar, combine all of the spices. Seal and shake well to combine.

· *tips* ·

To toast the fenugreek, place in a dry pan over medium heat and cook, stirring constantly, for 2 to 3 minutes, until fragrant and lightly browned. Remove from pan immediately and let cool before grinding in a spice grinder or clean coffee grinder.

This recipe makes more spice mix than you will need for this dish. Cover and keep in a cool, dark place for up to 1 year.

If desired, you can substitute a store-bought berbere spice mix.

Goodness is sharing,
listening, participating ...
being present with family
and friends over a table, at a
meal. Food connects us and
brings us goodness (love).

Arlene Stein

Keith Froggett

Executive chef & co-owner
• Scaramouche •
Toronto, ON

Hometown: Westgate-on-Sea, Kent, EN

He will tell you that he's the kind of chef who is happiest in the kitchen, working alongside his team to create beautiful dishes that look like exquisite gems on a plate. What he's less likely to talk about is how he's one of the most generous restaurateurs in the country. It's just not Keith Froggett's style to trumpet his achievements—and there are a great many of them.

Aside from what is well known about Keith and his work—more than 30 years in the business, Scaramouche listed among the top 50 restaurants in the world—he's a man who steps up to the plate whenever he is called upon to help. More than 11 years ago, Nick Saul, then the director of The Stop in Toronto, sent Keith an elegant letter explaining the vision he had for the organization.

"Nick is a very infectious guy, very compelling—and very persuasive," the British chef recalls. "I really like that organization and what they do. I like the way they treat people and that The Stop just isn't a food bank. They get people involved in their own destiny, get them growing their own food and giving them access to community ovens. It's a very cool way to serve a community."

The coming together of Nick and Keith resulted in an annual fundraising dinner at Scaramouche. It's a perfect mash-up: hungry diners in the front of house, and Scaramouche cooks volunteering their time cooking with volunteers from The Stop kitchens in the back. "It's a really nice way to raise funds for a great organization," adds Keith. "The Stop is like a small community within a city. And cities are made up of many. That's what keeps them vibrant."

Keith also supports the Georgetown Hospital in Halton Hills, Ontario, where he and his family once lived, as well as the Canadian Foundation for AIDS Research (CANFAR), Action Against Hunger's Love Food Give Food campaign, and Gold Medal Plates (net proceeds to the Canadian Olympic Foundation), to name just a few.

When asked about his philanthropy, Keith has a simple explanation: "That's just the type of person I am. You do need to give back. If no one does anything, what kind of community are we living in?" His generous nature is also evident in his kitchen. He has helped shape some of Canada's best chefs and taught them to respect the integrity of their ingredients. It's that—not the critical accolades, or Scaramouche topping "best of" lists again, or even having cooked for food royalty like Alain Ducasse and Julia Child—which gives him the greatest joy these days. Keith loves to see people thrive and to bask in the camaraderie that happens in the kitchen. He considers his staff and former cooks extended family.

If his life had turned out just a little differently, he may have been a carpenter. At the same time as he had an interview for enrollment in a college culinary arts program, he interviewed to become a woodworker. "I was never a good student," he recalls. "I did know I was going to do something with my hands." Cooking and the wealth of travel opportunities it offered won out. When he first started cooking, he was amazed at the bounty of new ideas and experiences at his feet. "I just fell into it," he says modestly. "And once you're in, it's difficult to get out. I think I've been really fortunate, and I have not looked back."

Most of us are quite fortunate in our lives. But there's not much in between living comfortably and not comfortably these days. If we say to those people who are struggling, "It's not my problem," where would we be?

keith froggett

This quiche is something my family and I look forward to sharing each spring. It is a happy coincidence that the first fire morels coming out of British Columbia coincide with the arrival of the wild leeks in the woods on our property in Caledon, Ontario. The kitchen is redolent with the aromas of this dish as it bakes gently in the oven.

wild leek & morel quiche

makes one 9-inch quiche

1 9-inch tart ring, lined with pie pastry and prebaked

1 tbsp vegetable oil

2 oz double smoked bacon, diced

3 oz fresh morels, split lengthwise (see Tip)

Sea salt and freshly ground black pepper

4 oz small wild leeks, coarsely sliced

1 tsp chopped fresh thyme

2 oz aged white cheddar cheese, shredded

1 oz Parmigiano-Reggiano cheese, grated

5 large eggs, at room temperature

¼ cup whipping (35%) cream

¼ cup whole milk

1 Preheat the oven to 325°F.

2 In a skillet over medium heat, heat oil. Add bacon and cook for a few moments, until fragrant. Add morels, season with salt and pepper to taste, and continue cooking until mushrooms are lightly browned and have given up any liquid they contain (which won't be much), 4 to 5 minutes.

3 Add leeks and thyme; continue cooking until leeks are limp and tender, about 2 minutes.

4 Remove from heat and check seasoning; adjust as necessary. Spread mixture evenly over prebaked pastry crust. Sprinkle with cheeses. Set aside.

5 In a bowl, beat eggs, then whisk in cream and milk. Season with salt and pepper to taste. Pour over cheeses and mushroom mixture in the tart ring.

6 Bake on the middle rack of the preheated oven until just set (start checking at about 20 minutes; quiche should be slightly wobbly in the centre). Remove from heat and let cool slightly. Serve warm or at room temperature.

· *tip* ·

To clean mushrooms, simply wipe them with a damp paper towel. Don't wash with water, as the mushrooms will absorb it.

I am not really a fan of dessert, but ... this is the type of dessert I love: small, rich, and packs a punch of flavours and textures.

panna cotta

serves 6

4 sheets leaf gelatin

1¼ cups whipping (35%) cream

¾ cup granulated sugar

1 cup milk

¾ cup plain yogurt

Vincotto (see Tip)

1 Place gelatin in a small bowl and cover with cold water. Set aside until soft, about 5 minutes.

2 Meanwhile, in a saucepan, combine cream and sugar. Bring to a boil, reduce heat, and simmer, stirring occasionally, until sugar is completely dissolved. Remove from heat and let cool slightly.

3 Lift out soaked gelatin and squeeze to remove excess water (discard soaking liquid). Add soaked gelatin to cream mixture and stir until it is completely dissolved. Let cool for a few minutes and then add milk and yogurt, stirring to combine.

4 Pour into suitable serving glasses and refrigerate for 2 to 3 hours to set.

5 Serve cold topped with seasonal berries drizzled with vincotto.

· tip ·

Vincotto means "cooked wine," and it is a dark, sweet, flavourful condiment made by slow-cooking red wine grapes until reduced and concentrated. You can find it in well-stocked artisanal food markets. If you can't find any, you can substitute high-quality balsamic vinegar.

Kim Fox

Director of programming & innovation
NDG Food Depot
Montreal, QC

Hometown: Etobicoke, ON

As an artist and painter, Kim Fox never thought her interest in food, politics, human rights, and creativity could ever converge. But she's found a sweet spot at the NDG Food Depot in the Notre-Dame-de-Grâce (aka NDG) area of Montreal, in the city's west end. Here, she can put in motion new and innovative programs to support participants in their efforts to eat better, lead, learn, share, and knit tighter bonds as a community.

Prevailing in the workshops and programs is a can-do attitude, one of "Let's try it!" Despite having only a small kitchen equipped with regular stoves, like the kind you'd find in any Montreal household, Kim and volunteer chef Brian Lott decided to launch a community meal program.

"It didn't matter that we didn't have all the resources or equipment we needed," says Kim. "We saw a need and a desire, so we made it happen." The meal program started small and slow with just 50 participants, then grew to a point where as many as 250 people are being served over a 4-hour period on Mondays and Fridays from the volunteer-run kitchen.

The program's success has had a profound effect on the NDG Food Depot, and Kim couldn't be more pleased: "Our space has really changed. It has become a lively meeting space. Everyone eats together and talks." The depot takes a pragmatic approach to food. Although it offers emergency food baskets to meet immediate needs, with its meal program, it goes much further. Kim puts a lot of focus on learning, so the fresh ingredients used in the community meal are also the ones found in the baskets, and recipes are offered to participants.

Community gardens, an affordable fresh-food market, and cooking classes are all part of the mix at the Depot, in hopes that when participants come through the door initially for a meal or a food basket, they will one day become involved, whether it's by taking a class on how to grow seedlings for their garden or by helping to prepare and serve meals to their fellow community members.

If there's one thing that makes Kim feel like she's in the perfect job, it's seeing self-determination in action: "I love to see how proud people are when they take the opportunity to lead a cooking class, teaching others to make one of their favourite recipes. Doing it their way. There's so much joy in the kitchen—talking, laughing, and sharing."

Kim's path to NDG was forged when she put her career as an artist on hold in order to return to school to study politics at Concordia University. During a class about the globalization of food, she had an *aha!* moment that sparked a desire to learn more about food systems. She went on to organize a series of events around food issues at Concordia and co-founded City Farm School, a training program for growing food in cities. She then spent 2 years in Toronto working with the Centre for Food Studies at Ryerson, co-writing the history of Foodshare and honing her skills as a gardener. In November 2013, she leapt at the chance to become a garden and kitchen coordinator at the NDG Food Depot.

> There is so much great work happening, so much momentum, and so much more good work to be done. The sky's the limit.

Ever since, Kim has been using her creativity to enrich the experiences of the depot's participants. "I love that I get to talk with people from all walks of life. I learn so much. It's a very dynamic job. And, as we evolve as an organization, I get to try out more new ideas. Plus, I get to eat a lot of great food. I love all those things. I feel very lucky."

kim fox

Delicious for breakfast, lunch, or dinner, this smoky, sweet, and savoury dish is my twist on the more traditional Tunisian and Israeli favourite. I love to serve it with toasted grainy bread topped with butter, but it can also be served atop your favourite grain.

smoky chakchouka

serves 2 to 3

1 tbsp oil

1 medium onion, cut into ½- to 1-inch pieces

2 red, orange, or yellow bell peppers, seeded and cut into ½- to 1-inch pieces

3 medium tomatoes or ⅔ can (28 oz) diced tomatoes, drained

2 small or 1 large clove garlic, minced

1 chipotle pepper in adobo sauce, chopped, plus 1 tbsp sauce

1 handful fresh basil leaves, chopped

Sea salt and freshly ground black pepper

4 to 6 eggs

1 In a large skillet over medium heat, heat oil. Add onion and sauté until soft and translucent, 3 to 4 minutes.

2 Add bell peppers and cook until softened, 2 to 3 minutes. Stir in tomatoes, garlic, and chipotle and sauce and simmer for 7 to 10 minutes, until mixture has thickened slightly. Stir in basil.

3 Using the back of a spoon, make 4 to 6 hollows (depending on how many eggs you are serving) in the mixture. Crack eggs into hollows, giving each egg as much room as possible in the pan. Cook for 5 to 7 minutes, until egg whites start to solidify, then cover the pan with a lid. Cook for about 5 minutes, until tops of eggs cook (you want eggs to be cooked through but without the yolks completely solidifying; they should still run a bit when pierced). Season with salt and pepper to taste.

4 Remove from heat and serve immediately.

These bowls require a bit more prep work but the components can be made throughout the week and refrigerated until ready to use. This recipe is inspired in part by my good friends at Burritoville in Montreal.

burrito bowl

serves 6 to 8

sweet & spicy black bean mixture

1 tbsp oil

1 small onion, diced

2 small or 1 large apple, cored and diced

2 tsp chili powder

1 tsp ground cumin

2 cups cooked or canned black beans, rinsed and drained

1 tomato, diced

Sea salt and freshly ground black pepper

1 In a deep pan or wide pot over medium heat, heat oil. Add onion and sauté until translucent, 3 to 4 minutes.

2 Stir in apple and cook for 3 to 5 minutes, until crisp-tender.

3 Reduce heat to medium-low and stir in chili powder and cumin. Cook, stirring frequently, for 1 to 2 minutes, until fragrant.

4 Add beans and tomato. Cover and reduce heat to low. Simmer for 10 to 15 minutes to let the flavours meld.

5 Uncover and cook for 2 to 3 minutes, until sauce has thickened slightly.

6 Season with salt and pepper to taste. Let cool, cover, and refrigerate until ready to use. Warm before using.

roasted sweet potatoes

1 large or 2 medium sweet potatoes, cut into 1-inch cubes

1 tbsp olive oil

Sea salt and freshly ground black pepper

1 Preheat the oven to 400°F. Lightly grease a baking sheet.

2 In a large bowl, toss together potatoes, oil, and salt and pepper to taste (feel free to get creative here and add your favourite spice).

3 Spread potatoes evenly on the prepared baking sheet, being careful not to crowd them. Bake in the preheated

continued…

oven until slightly brown and crisp, about 40 minutes (flip potatoes halfway through cooking time for an even bake). Remove from the oven. Let cool, cover, and refrigerate until ready to use. Warm before using.

spicy slaw

3 tbsp mayonnaise (see Tips)

Juice of 2 limes

1 chipotle pepper in adobo, finely chopped, plus 1½ tbsp sauce

½ medium sweet or red onion, finely diced (see Tips)

1 tsp garlic salt

1 handful fresh cilantro leaves, finely chopped

2 large carrots, grated

½ medium red cabbage, halved and cut into very thin strips

½ medium green cabbage, halved and cut into very thin strips

1 In a bowl, combine mayonnaise, lime juice, chipotle and sauce, onion, garlic salt, and cilantro.

2 In another bowl, combine carrots and cabbage. Pour mayonnaise mixture overtop and toss to combine. Cover and refrigerate until ready to use.

· tips ·

You can substitute 2 tbsp olive oil mixed with lime juice to taste, for the mayonnaise.

For a mellower flavour, rinse sliced onion under cool running water before using.

avocado cream

1 ripe avocado, halved and pitted

4 tbsp plain yogurt or sour cream

1 tbsp minced sweet onion or 1 tsp garlic salt

Juice of 1 lime

1 tsp jalapeño Tabasco (optional)

Sea salt

1 Scoop avocado flesh into a bowl and mash with a fork. Add yogurt, onion, lime juice, and Tabasco (if using) and stir to combine. Season with salt to taste. Cover and refrigerate until ready to use.

salsa

1 can (28 oz) diced tomatoes or 4 tomatoes, diced, with juice

1 small sweet or red onion, diced

1 handful fresh cilantro leaves, chopped

Juice of 1½ limes

½ jalapeño pepper, seeded and chopped, or to taste (see Tip)

Sea salt and freshly ground black pepper

1 In a bowl, combine tomatoes, onion, cilantro, lime juice, jalapeño, and salt and pepper to taste. Cover and refrigerate until ready to use. (Salsa is best if it's left to sit for about 2 hours in the refrigerator, for the flavours to meld, before serving.)

· tip ·

I usually use only one-quarter of a pepper, as it's quite spicy, but feel free to use as much as you like.

assembly

4 cups cooked rice (I prefer short-grain brown rice), warmed

1 Divide cooked rice among serving bowls (about ²/3 cup per bowl).

2 Top each bowl with ¹/3 cup spicy black beans, 1 cup spicy slaw, and ¹/3 cup roasted sweet potato, arranged in a triangle formation.

3 In the middle, place 1 heaping tbsp each avocado cream and salsa. If you have corn chips, stick a couple in the top to garnish. (Though how you dress your bowl is entirely up to you!)

Kristina McMillan

Director
NorWest Co-op
Community Food Centre
Winnipeg, MB

Hometown: Brandon, MB

The fifth Community Food Centre in Canada opened its doors in Winnipeg's Inkster neighbourhood in spring 2015, with Kristina McMillan at the helm. "In the first month, our numbers were through the roof," says Kristina. "They were bigger than we thought they would be. A lot of our programs were already at capacity. It's clear the need is definitely here."

For Kristina, working at NorWest is the culmination of all her previous experiences with food. She grew up in Brandon, Manitoba, a small agricultural town. Growing up there "drilled into me the importance of good food," she says. It prompted her to do a master's degree in Scotland, to look at the impact of food policies on the well-being of a community. "I started thinking more and more about how food shapes people's lives," she says.

Back in Canada, Kristina had a chance to put her education into action with Food Matters Manitoba, which, among other things, runs a program teaching youth where their food comes from. Then she joined NorWest. At the time, it was a health centre that offered very little when it came to food programming. Through the centre's partnership with Community Food Centres Canada, that void has been filled, and the facility has been able to take on food security as a health issue, with an integrated approach that involves doctors, nurses, social workers, and dieticians.

NorWest's food centre launched with 16 programs, from the Filipino Family Cooking Group to the After

School Smoothie Drop-In, many created as a result of community feedback. In the after-school drop-in, kids create healthy smoothies using pedal power: they hop on specially modified bicycles fitted with a blender jar, and the faster

We have a lot of supporters— volunteers and donors—who share our philosophy: Healthy food is a right.

they cycle, the more the blender blades whirr. The program is a great example of meeting the need for good food in a fun, interactive way. The idea is to start educating young taste buds early. "If we don't, by the time they become adults, the kids have become accustomed to high-fat, high-salt prepackaged foods," Kristina says.

Kristina has had some remarkable moments at the Community Food Centre. She was there to see a 10-year-old boy try spinach for the first time. He picked a leaf out of the salad on his plate and asked, "Is this food?" She has also witnessed a shift in the once very divided neighbourhood, where residents in social housing, members of First Nations, new Canadians, and seniors did not mingle. NorWest is changing that. Thanks in part to the round tables in the dining room that encourage discussion, the divide is shrinking.

"The kitchen brings together people who would never have had a chance to interact before," she explains. "Food is the commonality. It's the hook. We all like good food. There is a huge opportunity to build a stronger community around that. Seeing the buy-in has been the most rewarding part for me. It creates an entirely different feeling for the centre when you have the neighbourhood actively engaged in bettering their health. We want to help create change and lead by example."

This recipe uses pickerel, a local Manitoba fish also known as walleye,
but any mild-flavoured fish pairs well with the tropical flavours of the salsa.
Serve with wild rice and a crisp green salad alongside.

baked pickerel with mango salsa

serves 2 to 3

⅓ cup olive oil

1 tbsp fresh lemon juice

1 clove garlic

1 tbsp chopped fresh flat-leaf
parsley leaves

1 tsp chopped fresh basil leaves

1 tsp freshly ground black pepper

4 to 6 pickerel fillets

1 large mango, peeled, pitted,
and cut into small dice

1 jalapeño pepper, seeded
and finely chopped

½ red bell pepper, seeded
and cut into small dice

2 tbsp fresh lime juice

1 tbsp fresh lemon juice

1 tbsp chopped fresh
cilantro leaves

Sea salt and freshly ground
black pepper

1 In a bowl, combine oil, lemon juice, garlic, parsley, basil, and pepper.

2 Place fillets in a resealable bag or airtight container. Pour marinade over fish. Seal or cover and gently turn to coat. Refrigerate for 1 hour.

3 Preheat the oven to 350°F.

4 Transfer fish to a lightly greased baking dish (discard marinade). Bake in the preheated oven for 20 to 30 minutes, until fish is opaque and flakes easily with a fork.

5 Meanwhile, in a bowl, combine mango, jalapeño, red pepper, lime juice, lemon juice, cilantro, and salt and pepper.

6 To serve, divide fish among serving plates. Top with mango salsa.

Poached pears in red wine is pure heaven. This is a traditional Italian recipe made with simple ingredients. Chef Anna Paganelli of De Luca's in Winnipeg shared the preparation with me. I had the pleasure of working alongside Anna for a few years, and she taught me that if you use quality ingredients in your recipes, the flavours will absolutely sing.

poached pears in red wine

serves 6

6 ripe Bosc pears, unpeeled, halved and cored

1 lemon, sliced

1 cinnamon stick

2 cups dry red wine

½ cup granulated sugar

Vanilla ice cream or gelato

1 Place pears in a large saucepan, skin side up, and cover with water. Add lemon and cinnamon stick. Bring to a boil over medium heat. Cover, reduce the heat, and simmer for 15 to 20 minutes, until pears are cooked but still firm.

2 Drain pears, reserving cinnamon stick. Return pears to pan, skin side up, along with reserved cinnamon stick. Pour in wine and sugar. Simmer over medium heat, uncovered, until liquid has reduced slightly and thickened, about 15 minutes. Remove from heat and let cool slightly.

3 Divide pears among serving plates. Serve with a scoop of vanilla ice cream in the centre of each pear. Drizzle with wine syrup.

Lil MacPherson

Founder, co-owner & activist
• The Wooden Monkey •
Halifax & Dartmouth, NS

Hometown: Dartmouth, NS

Anyone who has met Lil MacPherson, a leading food activist, will admit that it's nearly impossible not to be swept up in her zeal. She lives and breathes to spread the word about the frailty of our planet and the food system it supports. From overseeing a successful restaurant to donating food to soup kitchens and embarking on public-speaking tours, she is focused on educating the world one person, one bite, at a time.

Her food career started early. She was an ice-cream super-scooper at a factory, waitressed at age 16, then worked at a big mcfast-food restaurant. She graduated to opening restaurants for other people, but the experience left her dissatisfied. "I just couldn't serve that kind of food to people anymore. I wanted to follow my passion for organic and macrobiotic food," she says. "I left a really good job and took a pay cut for a job at an organic bakery. Then along came Juan."

The Juan in question was the devastating hurricane that swept through Nova Scotia and the Eastern Seaboard in 2003. "It scared the crap out of me. I was sitting alone in my house in the dark thinking about how we are doing as a province. I was thinking about climate change and the fact that we wait for 90 percent of our food to come to us. It made me sick that it was so difficult to get organic food. I wondered, 'What can I do to change things?' I knew restaurants very well, so that was a good place to start."

Although she and her longtime business partner Christine Bower (restaurant manger extraordinaire) didn't have the money or backing to start their own restaurant, they were nevertheless determined to open one that would focus on using locally sourced non-GMO and organic ingredients whenever possible, incorporate the principles of macrobiotic cooking, and be kind to the planet. And it would cater to everyone, from vegans to carnivores and those in between, in hopes of moving "organic" out of the hippie realm and into the mainstream. They borrowed equipment anywhere they could, and decorated the space with mismatched chairs and whatever else they could find.

People. Planet. Profit. Those are the priorities. "It was a massive leap of faith," says Lil. "But I was more scared of not doing it than I was of failing."

Lil had to drag their first customer at the restaurant in off the street. And in those early days, they had only a couple of farm suppliers. These days, the tables at both locations of The Wooden Monkey are busy, filled with eclectic clientele drawn to good food (with ingredients from 18 suppliers now) and good politics, thanks also to her partners Christine Bower and Matthew Gass.

From ice-cream scooper to in-demand lecturer who flies all over the world to talk climate change and food issues, it has been a crazy dream come true for Lil, and she couldn't be more pleased. Yet despite the speaking engagements, her community involvement, supporting international and domestic charities, and operating what she calls "a restaurant with a conscience," she's not content.

Now she wants to go a step beyond and herself produce the good food she knows to be so important. She'll have that opportunity with the 40-acre farm she purchased near Tatamagouche. "I'm becoming a farmer!" she exclaims. "I sold my motorcycle and bought a tractor. My friends think I'm crazy, but they understand."

Thanks to her wonderful partners, she'll be taking a summer off from her restaurants to learn how to grow food on her swath of land—her idea of paradise. "I'm so close to nature now," she says, "that I'd take a bullet for a cricket."

> *It's important for me to bring my values to my job. I think it's my duty. I think every businessperson should be involved in their community.*

Beets are the liver's best friend! And our liver could use our help: it processes everything put into the body, including medications, food additives, and water and air pollutants. So be good to your liver and eat beets!

roasted beet, aged gouda & pickled onion salad

serves 4

roasted beets

1 lb small mixed beets, trimmed and scrubbed

2 tbsp olive oil

Sea salt and freshly ground black pepper

4 cups mixed salad greens

Organic Apple Cider Vinaigrette (recipe follows)

2 oz Gouda cheese, shaved

Pickled Onions (recipe follows)

1 Preheat the oven to 350°F.

2 In a large bowl, toss beets with oil until well coated. Season with salt and pepper to taste. Transfer to a large baking dish.

3 Roast in the preheated oven for 35 minutes, or until tender (if beets are large, they may take up to 1 hour). Remove from heat and let cool.

4 When cool enough to handle, using your fingers (wear gloves, if desired, to prevent staining your hands), slip skins off beets (discard skin). Cut larger beets in half or quarters, if necessary.

5 In a large serving bowl, combine cooled beets with mixed greens. Add vinaigrette to taste and toss to coat well.

6 Divide among serving plates. Sprinkle with shaved Gouda and pickled onions to taste.

continued…

organic apple cider vinaigrette

makes about 1½ cups

1 cup extra-virgin olive oil

¼ cup organic apple cider

3 tbsp organic cider vinegar

2 tbsp whole-grain mustard

2 tbsp liquid honey

Pinch fine sea salt and freshly ground black pepper

1 Place all ingredients in a blender and blend on high speed until well incorporated.

pickled onions

serves 4

1 cup white vinegar

1 cup cane sugar

1 tsp whole black peppercorns

½ tsp sea salt

1 sprig fresh thyme

12 mini red onions, quartered

1 In a saucepan over medium heat, combine vinegar, sugar, peppercorns, salt, and thyme. Bring to a boil. Add onions and cook until just tender, about 8 minutes. Remove from heat and let cool.

2 Transfer onions and cooking liquid to a resealable jar. Cover and refrigerate for at least 24 hours before using.

Goodness is simply
the absence of evil or
maliciousness. Or anything
that makes you smile.

Kristine Stone

North Americans are starting to realize what people in the rest of the world have always known: all parts of lamb are edible and, when prepared correctly, they can be so delicious. At The Wooden Monkey, we love to use lamb shanks. We're happy to see that the cut is becoming more popular.

savoury braised lamb shanks *with* barley risotto

serves 4

lamb shanks

1 tbsp oil

4 lamb shanks (1 to 1¼ lb each)

Sea salt and freshly ground black pepper

1 large onion, cut into ¼-inch dice

3 carrots, cut into ¼-inch dice

3 ribs celery, cut into ¼-inch dice

1 leek, white and green parts, cut into ¼-inch dice

1 sweet potato, cut into ¼-inch dice

4 cloves garlic, minced

1 can (6 oz) tomato paste

3 bay leaves

1 tbsp chopped fresh rosemary

1 tsp minced fresh thyme leaves

2 cups port

4 cups vegetable stock

1 Preheat the oven to 350°F.

2 In a large skillet over medium heat, heat oil. Season lamb shanks with salt and pepper to taste and cook until brown on all sides, about 5 minutes per side. Transfer browned shanks to a plate.

3 To the same pan, add onion, carrots, celery, leek, and sweet potato and cook until lightly browned, about 5 minutes.

4 Stir in garlic and tomato paste and cook for about 2 minutes, until garlic is fragrant. Stir in bay leaves, rosemary, and thyme. Add port, stirring to scrape up any browned bits from the bottom of the pan, and cook until liquid has reduced by half, about 5 minutes.

5 Return browned shanks to pan. Add just enough stock to cover shanks (they should be submerged). Cover pan with aluminum foil and place in the pre-heated oven. Roast for 2½ to 3 hours, turning over halfway through cooking time, until shanks are tender and cooked through. Remove foil for the last 15 minutes of cooking.

continued…

barley risotto

1 tbsp oil

1 shallot, diced

1 clove garlic, minced

2 tbsp dry white wine

½ cup whipping
(35%) cream

1 tbsp chopped fresh
flat-leaf parsley

2 cups cooked pot barley

¼ cup freshly grated
Parmesan cheese

Sea salt and freshly ground
black pepper

1 In a skillet over medium heat, heat oil. Add shallot and garlic and sauté until lightly brown, about 4 minutes. Add wine and bring to a boil, scraping up any browned bits from the bottom of the pan. Stir in cream and parsley, and return to a boil.

2 Stir in barley and cheese. Cook until barley absorbs cooking liquid and becomes thick and creamy. Season with salt and pepper to taste. Keep warm until ready to serve.

assembly

1 To serve, divide barley risotto among serving plates. Top with braised lamb shank. Enjoy!

· tip ·

Barley may be one of the oldest grains on earth, but it's not one that is used as often as it should be. It is a nutritional powerhouse, stabilizing the body's blood glucose levels and providing both cardiovascular protection and cancer prevention. This ancient whole grain satisfies more than just our palate!

Each person has
inside a basic decency
and goodness. If he
listens to it and acts on
it, he is giving a great
deal of what it is the
world needs most.

Pablo Casals

Liz Anderson

Community action coordinator
The Local Community Food Centre
Stratford, ON

Hometown: Toronto, ON

Long before Liz Anderson took a job at The Local, she had already heard about the tremendous strides that The Stop in Toronto was making in assisting people on low incomes. It was the first organization of its kind and would serve as a template for more Community Food Centre locations, including in Stratford. "The Stop was pretty notorious, in a really good way," she says. "They were very influential. I knew what I was getting into."

The Local launched in November 2012. Over the two years she spent at The Local, Liz has seen both the Community Food Centre and the people who use it flourish. In her role, she helps them to find their voice, to exercise their right to good food, and to be treated as valuable members of society. The first step in achieving all this is surprisingly simple: eating a good, nutritious meal. The rest follows.

"If people come in, they will come in for a meal," Liz explains. "They find an atmosphere of friendliness and acceptance. It starts with food." She has seen first-hand the hesitation of some who come through the door. They expect the usual—having to stand in a soup line in a dark, dingy basement. The Local is quite the opposite, Liz points out. "It's bright and sunny. It has a real community vibe. It's an exciting and empowering place to be. People can sit down and have a meal brought to them at the table. We don't want people lining up. In dealing with social service agencies, they are always lining up. We don't want that kind of atmosphere. This is so astoundingly different."

The centre has a healthy-food policy: everything, from perogies to sauces, is made from scratch. Good food makes people feel valued. The centre's clients can also connect with peer advocates, who talk with them about how they are doing and offer help, including explaining rights around income support. That's a conversation starter: people start to think about the bigger picture; they realize that justice issues go beyond the individual."

The beauty of peer advocates is that, as members of the same community, they truly understand the issues and challenges. Liz works with them to boost participation in the various programs offered, from Loving Spoonfuls (nutrition classes for moms-to-be) to a social justice club. One of the projects undertaken by this club was Campaign 226, named for the number of families in Stratford on the waiting list for social housing in November 2014.

Liz and members of the campaign's committee went to the open budget meeting held by the municipality. The town councillors planned on increasing the budget for social housing by $50,000, but after talking to them, the committee managed to increase that amount by $36,000. It was a huge victory. "Wins like this give people hope," Liz says. "They can see our culture of activism and empowerment. People who were passive and marginalized rediscover their power and value. Now they are agents of change."

Liz has witnessed other wins too—a woman with thoughts of suicide finding joy in working in The Local's

> **My greatest reward is seeing people take strides forward—a result of the community we have built.**

greenhouse, youth groups cooking together to make food to take home to their families, a woman who went from being thoroughly intimidated speaking at a meeting of the social justice club to organizing Campaign 226 and serving as its spokesperson, then enrolling in a college program to further her goal of becoming a social service worker.

"For some people, it was the first time they had done anything political. For others, it was the first time they stood up and said, 'No. This isn't okay. We are valuable members of this community and our needs are not being met.' It's incredible to see. I'm so grateful for an opportunity to be a part of the change."

liz anderson

My partner is a cheese professional, so cheese is a big part of my diet. Fondue is one of my favourite things about winter in snowy Stratford. This recipe is a twist on the original Swiss dish. Serve in a fondue pot, if you have one, with slices of apples, pears, and roasted potatoes.

canadian cheese fondue

serves 4

1½ cups shredded cheddar cheese

1½ cups shredded Oka cheese

2 to 3 tbsp all-purpose flour (we prefer a gluten-free blend)

1 cup hard cider

Splash Canadian whisky

2 cloves garlic, minced

Freshly ground black pepper

Pinch nutmeg

1 In a bowl, combine cheeses and toss with flour.

2 In a saucepan over medium heat, warm cider until hot (do not boil). Stir in whisky and garlic. Add cheese mixture a handful at a time, stirring constantly, until cheese is completely melted and bubbling.

3 Remove from heat and season with pepper to taste and nutmeg. Serve immediately.

My partner's family makes these rich and fudgy gluten-free brownies for me on special occasions. Sometimes dessert gets overlooked for people who don't eat gluten, so I really appreciate it! If you like, you can omit the almonds.

the *best* gluten-free brownies

makes one 8- x 8-inch square pan of brownies

⅓ cup almond flour

⅓ cup gluten-free flour blend

1 tsp baking powder

½ tsp sea salt

3 to 5 oz semisweet chocolate, chopped

½ cup butter

1 cup raw sugar

2 whole eggs

1 egg yolk

1 tsp pure vanilla extract

1 cup semisweet chocolate chips

¾ cup toasted almonds

1 Preheat the oven to 350°F. Lightly grease an 8- × 8-inch square baking pan.

2 In a mixing bowl, combine almond flour, gluten-free flour blend, baking powder, and salt. Set aside.

3 In a double boiler or a heatproof bowl placed over a saucepan of simmering water, combine chocolate and butter, stirring until completely melted and smooth. Remove from heat and let cool.

4 To chocolate, add sugar, eggs and egg yolk, and vanilla and stir until combined. Add dry ingredients and stir until smooth. Fold in chocolate chips and almonds. Spread mixture evenly into prepared baking pan.

5 Bake in preheated oven for 30 to 35 minutes or until a few moist crumbs cling to a toothpick inserted in the centre. Remove from oven and let cool in pan.

6 Cut into squares and enjoy.

Chef
Ruby WatchCo.
Toronto, ON

Hometown: Bailieboro, ON

There was never any question about Lora Kirk becoming a chef. Growing up on a farm near Peterborough, Ontario, she learned early on to respect good ingredients and how they are served.

It's a philosophy she brings to her kitchen at Ruby WatchCo. in Toronto, and to the many events she supports locally, from Restaurants for Change (to benefit Community Food Centres Canada) to grassroots causes like Not Far from the Tree (where volunteers pick fruit from Toronto-area trees and pass it along to the trees' owners and to food banks).

Lora's out to spread her love of producers and growers. She can't help but be enthusiastic. Her childhood was filled with fresh eggs, pickles made lovingly by her grandmother, and vegetables that landed on the supper table just hours after being plucked from the garden. "When you work so hard to grow something, you truly appreciate it," Lora says. "You wouldn't dare waste a thing."

That was sometimes learned the hard way. She recalls the time she and her brother carelessly spilled a week's supply of milk from her aunt Joyce's cow. As punishment, her mother made them drink powdered milk for a while. You can bet they never took that fresh milk for granted ever again. She also remembers the honey being extracted from combs in her grandmother's basement. The sweetness of it lighting up her young taste buds as she chewed the beeswax like gum is something she'll never forget.

As a chef who worked in London and New York before landing back in Canada, she loves that people now are developing that same kind of appreciation for ingredients. And it hasn't come solely out of better education or from the wealth of media coverage on locally grown produce. Lora sees tastiness as a strong ambassador. "Customers ask questions after they've tasted our food," she explains. "They say that their green beans or carrots don't taste the way they do in our restaurant. That gives us a chance to talk about where these vegetables came from and the need to support farmers in our community."

Lora is a loyal supporter of several local causes. "I don't do events for the sake of doing events," she says. "I want to know where the money is going, what's the goal of the event, and who else is going there. For me, it's not about getting my name out there. I do it for the charity or the cause that I want to be a part of."

> **When I talk to farmers, their excitement about what they are growing is infectious. I can't help but feel that way too.**

Even at large events, she gives farmers star treatment. She partners with local growers to showcase their produce and provides introductions to new customers, whether they are home cooks or celebrity chefs. It's how she rolls. At every meal she supports the men and women who grow, fish, and raise food.

Her latest endeavour is centred on cod from Fogo Island in Newfoundland. She's partnering with a handful of Toronto chefs to buy the fish regularly. It's not only an effort to put something special and delicious on the menu; it's a way to make a very real impact in the Atlantic community. She's excited about the prospect of helping up to 20 families once again support themselves and make a living from fishing and processing cod.

Although she works with top chefs like Lynn Crawford and Gordon Ramsay, it's these moments of creating positive change in the lives of the people who provide us with food that makes her love what she does more than anything else in the world.

183 *lora kirk*

This delicious twist on bacon and eggs makes a satisfying brunch or dinner. The green goddess dressing provides a nice creamy, herby contrast to the crispy pork belly and eggs, and the brown derby vinaigrette adds a nice tang to the fresh greens.

crispy egg & pork belly salad with green goddess dressing

serves 6

Green Goddess Dressing (recipe follows)

12 Crispy Pork Belly Strips (recipe follows)

6 Crispy Eggs (recipe follows)

2 bunches watercress

2 heads frisée, torn

3 garden radishes, thinly sliced into coins

1 small cucumber, thinly sliced

¼ cup Brown Derby Vinaigrette (recipe follows)

Sea salt and freshly ground black pepper

1 Prepare green goddess dressing, crispy pork belly strips, and crispy eggs as directed.

2 In a large bowl, toss together watercress, frisée, radishes, cucumber, and vinaigrette. Season with salt and pepper to taste.

3 Spoon an even amount of green goddess dressing onto each of 6 serving plates. Divide salad among plates. Arrange 2 strips of pork belly alongside each serving of salad. Top each with a crispy egg. Serve immediately.

continued…

green goddess dressing

makes about 3 cups

2 ripe avocados, pitted and peeled

½ cup mayonnaise

¼ cup sour cream

1 clove garlic

¼ cup loosely packed fresh
flat-leaf parsley leaves

1 tbsp finely chopped fresh chives

2 tbsp fresh lemon juice

Sea salt and freshly ground
black pepper

1 In a blender, combine avocados, mayonnaise, sour cream, garlic, parsley, chives, and lemon juice. Blend on high speed until smooth. Season with salt and pepper to taste. Refrigerate until ready to use.

crispy pork belly strips

2 ½ lb pork belly

1 tbsp table salt

1 tsp baking powder

2 tbsp sea salt, divided

½ tsp cumin seeds

½ tsp coriander seeds

½ tsp fennel seeds

½ tsp chili flakes

2 tsp fresh thyme leaves

1 tbsp olive oil

1 bunch fresh rosemary

2 heads garlic, halved

2 lemons, halved

1 orange, quartered

1 Using a sharp knife, score skin of pork belly in ¼-inch intervals.

2 In a small bowl, combine table salt and baking powder. Rub into scored pork belly skin. Place seasoned pork belly in a roasting pan and refrigerate overnight, uncovered.

3 Preheat the oven to 350°F.

4 Place 1 tbsp sea salt, cumin seeds, coriander seeds, fennel seeds, chili flakes, thyme, and oil in a mortar and pestle and pound until well combined. Rub spice mixture all over pork belly. Roast, skin side up, in the preheated oven for 2 hours.

5 Remove the pan from the oven. Carefully transfer pork belly to a plate. In the bottom of the roasting pan, arrange rosemary, then garlic and lemon and orange pieces, cut side up. Place pork belly on top. Increase the oven temperature to 425°F and continue to roast pork belly for 30 to 45 minutes, until skin is golden and crispy and meat is tender. Remove from the oven and let cool for 10 minutes before slicing into 12 equal strips.

crispy eggs

6 eggs

1 cup all-purpose flour

2 eggs, for breading

1 tsp water

1 cup panko bread crumbs

Oil, for frying

1 Gently lower 6 eggs into a large saucepan of boiling water. Reduce heat to medium and simmer for 6 minutes (for soft-boiled eggs). Drain. Transfer boiled eggs to a bowl and cover with cold water. Set aside until cool, then very gently peel eggs.

2 Prepare breading station: In a shallow bowl, place flour. In another shallow bowl, whisk together 2 eggs and water. Place panko in a third shallow bowl.

3 Working with 1 soft-boiled egg at a time, gently roll in flour, then in egg mixture, then in panko. Place on a rimmed baking sheet.

4 Fill a large saucepan with 2 inches oil. Attach a deep-fry thermometer to the side of the pan. Heat oil to 375°F.

5 Working in two batches, fry breaded eggs, turning occasionally, until brown, about 2 minutes. Using a slotted spoon, transfer fried eggs to an ovenproof plate and place in a preheated 350°F oven for 3 minutes to heat through. Set aside, keeping warm, until ready to use.

brown derby vinaigrette

½ cup red wine vinegar

2 tsp balsamic vinegar

2 tbsp liquid honey

2 tbsp Dijon mustard

1 tbsp Worcestershire sauce

¼ tsp sea salt

Juice of 1 lemon (about 2 tbsp)

1⅓ cups canola oil

1 In a medium bowl, whisk together vinegars, honey, Dijon, Worcestershire sauce, salt, and lemon juice until well combined. Slowly whisk in oil until emulsified. Cover and refrigerate until ready to use. Store leftovers in an airtight container in the refrigerator and enjoy drizzled on fresh salad greens.

This moist, rich ginger-spiced cake is perfectly balanced by the addition of dark stout, mounds of fluffy orange meringue, and a drizzle of coffee caramel. We like to use Red Rocket Coffee Stout by Sawdust City Brewing.

ginger stout cake with *orange meringue & coffee caramel*

makes one 9- × 11-inch cake

2 cups stout beer

2 cups molasses

4 tbsp grated fresh gingerroot

1 tbsp baking soda

6 eggs

1 cup packed brown sugar

1 cup granulated sugar

1½ cups vegetable oil

4 cups all-purpose flour

1 tbsp baking powder

4 tbsp ground ginger

½ tbsp ground cinnamon

½ tsp ground cloves

½ tsp ground nutmeg

Orange Meringue (recipe follows)

Coffee Caramel (recipe follows)

1 Preheat the oven to 350°F. Grease a 9- × 11-inch cake pan.

2 In a large saucepan, combine stout, molasses, and fresh ginger and bring to a boil. Remove from heat, then stir in baking soda. Let sit until foam dissipates.

3 In a stand mixer fitted with the paddle attachment, or in a bowl using a wooden spoon, cream together eggs and sugars. Add oil and mix to combine.

4 In a bowl, sift together flour, baking powder, ground ginger, cinnamon, cloves, and nutmeg.

5 Add stout mixture to sugar mixture and mix until incorporated. Add flour mixture in two batches, mixing each batch until well incorporated. Pour batter into the prepared cake pan. Bake in the preheated oven for 30 to 35 minutes. Remove from the oven and let cool completely in the pan set on a wire rack.

6 Once cake is cool, turn out onto a serving plate. Decorate top of cake with orange meringue. Using a brûlé torch, caramelize meringue. Cut into portions and serve drizzled with coffee caramel.

continued…

orange meringue

4 large egg whites

1 cup granulated sugar

1 tsp grated orange zest

1 Using an electric mixer fitted with the whisk attachment, beat egg whites on medium speed until they hold soft peaks.

2 Increase speed to high. Add sugar, 1 tbsp at a time, continuing to beat until very stiff and shiny peaks form. Add orange zest and mix to combine.

coffee caramel

4 tsp instant coffee powder

8 tbsp water, divided

1⅓ cups granulated sugar

⅔ cup whipping (35%) cream

5 tbsp unsalted butter, diced

Pinch sea salt

1 In a small bowl, stir coffee powder with 2 tbsp water until dissolved.

2 In a heavy saucepan over low heat, combine remaining 6 tbsp water and sugar and heat, stirring, until sugar dissolves. Increase heat and boil mixture, without stirring but occasionally brushing down the sides of the pan with a pastry brush dipped into water and swirling the pan to prevent crystals from forming, until syrup turns deep amber, about 8 minutes.

3 Remove the pan from heat. Add cream, butter, and coffee (mixture will bubble vigorously). Return to heat and bring to a boil, whisking constantly until smooth. Whisk in salt. Set aside until ready to use.

Goodness means enjoying summer-fresh produce with great family and friends.

Susan Niczowski

Michael Ableman

Farmer, food activist & author
Salt Spring Island, BC

Hometown: Wilmington, Delaware

At the age of 18, Michael Ableman joined an agrarian commune—one that had 3,000 acres of farmland. At the time, Sunburst Farms was the largest organic producer and distributor in North America. Within a year of his arrival, he was managing a 100-acre pear and apple orchard. "After that experience, I had the fire," he remembers. "I looked around and wondered what I could do with my life—something that would not suck the life out of the world." He found his answer in farming.

Michael spent 30 years in California before heading north to Salt Spring Island, eventually farming on 120 acres of gorgeous land, a.k.a. Foxglove Farm. Of course, he uses it to grow beautiful organic fruits and vegetables and grains, but it's about more than that. It's about education.

Michael's passions come together at his Centre for Arts, Ecology & Agriculture, an innovative space offering workshops and retreats. He lectures on topics such as land stewardship, community well-being, and sustainable small- and medium-scale agriculture.

For more than 25 years, Michael has been inspiring a new generation of potential farmers through his Farm, Arts and Culinary Camp for Kids, geared to children ages 7 to 12. "It's important to get the kids out on the land—tasting, smelling, and seeing the incredibly dynamic nature of farms. The programming is almost secondary to just being here. This land is spectacular. You get out of your normal routine, for a day or a week or longer, and something magical happens."

At the same time, Michael is realistic about this romantic period we're currently in when it comes to farming: "Despite there being more books, films, and rock 'n' roll chefs talking about how much they love farmers and locally grown

food, the reality is that just 2 percent of the population are growing food for everyone else. There are a lot of spectators, but this isn't a spectator sport. When it comes right down to it, someone still needs to do the work."

In his spare time (insert chuckle here), the father-husband-farmer-educator-author-photographer spearheads Sole Food, a social enterprise created under the charity Cultivate Canada about six years ago to kick-start urban agriculture in Vancouver's gritty Downtown Eastside. It employs 25 residents—many with mental health issues or long-term addictions—who grow fresh produce for local markets and restaurants, with five acres of production done on pavement in boxes. Michael's involvement in urban agriculture began in the mid-1980s when he started the Center for Urban Architecture in California. But, true to his character, he didn't want to just talk about it. He wanted to roll up his sleeves and make it happen.

"I used to think that if I could beat people over the head with my message, be more eloquent in how I delivered it, things would change," Michael admits. "But then I realized I just needed to grow the best-tasting tomato. Pleasure is a much greater motivator than guilt will ever be. People eat it, then wonder, 'Why does this taste so good?' We set the table and extend the invitation, then everything else takes over. Anything I say or describe or teach is secondary."

It feels good just being out in the fields. It's so stimulating, and the quality of food is really exciting. I just love that we get to provide people with stuff that is so damn good.

193 *michael ableman*

Radicchio is one of those things that people either love or hate, although I suspect its controversial nature is tied to the fact that some folks have not embraced bitter as an acceptable note in their culinary repertoire. This recipe could convert even the most radicchio-resistant. The combination of the crispy, charred outer layer and the moist interior, and the bitter flavour combined with the sweet balsamic vinegar and the smoke from the grill, is amazing.

grilled radicchio with balsamic vinegar

serves 4 to 6

2 lb radicchio
(about 2 large heads)

1/3 cup olive oil

Kosher salt

Extra-virgin olive oil,
for drizzling

3 to 4 tbsp balsamic
vinegar

1 Prepare a fire in a charcoal grill or preheat a gas grill to high.

2 Remove bruised or wilted outer leaves from radicchio, then trim root end, leaving core intact. Cut radicchio into 1 1/2-inch-thick wedges and place in a large bowl. Drizzle with 1/3 cup olive oil, season generously with salt to taste, and toss to coat evenly.

3 Grill radicchio until underside is nicely browned and charred a little, 3 to 5 minutes. Turn and grill on other side for another 3 to 5 minutes, until radicchio is golden and tender.

4 Transfer to a serving platter and drizzle with extra-virgin olive oil and balsamic vinegar. Serve warm or at room temperature.

· tip ·

Radicchio that is especially dense benefits from being oiled and seasoned about 10 minutes before grilling.

Recipe excerpted from Michael Ableman's *Fields of Plenty: A Farmer's Journey in Search of Real Food and the People Who Grow It.* San Francisco: Chronicle Books, 2005. Reprinted by permission of the author.

Rich and earthy, this mash is delicious served with a
pat of butter and sprinkled with crunchy sea salt.

winter root mash

serves 4

1 medium celery root, peeled

1 large parsnip, peeled

½ lb Jerusalem artichokes
(about 7 small to medium
artichokes), peeled

2 medium parsley roots, peeled

Kosher salt

2 lb potatoes (about 3 large
potatoes) such as Yukon Gold
or Yellow Finn, peeled and
each cut into 8 pieces

¼ cup unsalted butter, softened,
plus extra for serving

½ cup heavy cream
(36% or higher), half-and-half,
or milk, warmed

Freshly cracked black pepper

Sea salt

1 Cut the celery root, parsnip, Jerusalem artichokes, and parsley roots into pieces of similar size and shape (about ¼ inch thick). Place in a medium saucepan and add water to cover by about 1 inch. Season with a generous amount of salt (the water should taste almost like seawater). Bring to a low boil, reduce heat, and simmer until all roots are completely tender when pierced with a knife, 25 to 30 minutes (be sure to check each variety of root vegetable). Drain. Spread roots in a single layer on a baking sheet and set aside in a warm place to dry for about 5 minutes.

2 Meanwhile, in a separate medium saucepan, add potatoes and water to cover by 1 inch. Season with a generous amount of salt (the water should taste almost like seawater). Bring to a low boil. Reduce heat and simmer until potatoes are completely tender when pierced with a knife, about 25 minutes. Drain. Spread potatoes in a single layer on a baking sheet and set aside in a warm place to dry for about 5 minutes.

3 While roots and potatoes are still warm, pass them through a food mill into a large bowl, along with butter. Stir in warm cream, just enough so purée reaches desired consistency. Season with pepper to taste and more kosher salt if necessary. Serve with a pat of butter sprinkled with crunchy sea salt to taste.

Recipe excerpted from Michael Ableman's *Fields of Plenty: A Farmer's Journey in Search of Real Food and the People Who Grow It.* San Francisco: Chronicle Books, 2005. Reprinted by permission of the author.

Mike Fata

CEO & co-founder
Manitoba Harvest Hemp Foods
Winnipeg, MB

Hometown: Winnipeg, MB

If there's anyone who understands the power of change, it's Mike Fata, an entrepreneur and health and social justice advocate. He's tapped into it both on a personal level and in business with a "do the right thing" attitude that includes working to boost the health of communities.

Healthy living is something he feels strongly about. As a teenager, he weighed 300 pounds. When he became "sick and tired of feeling sick and tired," he began a quest toward wellness that would take him through the hazardous world of fad diets to find out what worked and what didn't. After losing some weight but still experiencing the ill effects of a low-fat diet, he learned the importance of macro-nutrients. Through hemp foods Mike enjoyed the benefits of "good" omega fats, protein, and the right type of carbohydrates and lost over 100 pounds. And largely thanks to hemp foods, Mike has maintained his weight loss and feels better than ever.

But early on Canada wasn't quite ready to accept hemp foods (there were a lot of misconceptions around hemp and other plants within the cannabis family). Together with local farmers, academics, and provincial government officials, Mike and his co-founders educated on and successfully advocated for the legalization of industrial hemp in 1998. That cleared the way to start Manitoba Harvest and basically an entire industry. Today, more than 125 Western Canadian farmers are growing 50,000+ hemp acres annually. Manitoba Harvest employs over 100 people and offers a full range of hemp food products at over 7,000 retailers across North America.

Even in the early days, Mike had a clear vision for the company as one that would be kind to the planet and to those living on it. It started with food banks, helping to stock them with the healthy foods Manitoba Harvest manufactured. As the company flourished so did its philanthropic efforts, adding soup kitchens, shelters, the United Way, Red Cross, Habitat for Humanity, and others into the mix of organizations it supported.

When NorWest Co-op Community Food Centre opened in Winnipeg, Manitoba Harvest was a founding sponsor, fortifying its commitment to making good food more accessible. It recognizes the importance of education in the centre's programming, from cooking classes for single dads to a low-cost healthy-food market.

"We also think it's important for our team members to be involved in the community," says Mike. "They are paid for the time off they take to volunteer, whether it's lending a hand at a soup kitchen or picking up trash to make our streets cleaner and greener." It's all part of being a business that uses its power to solve social and environmental problems—one of the founding principles of becoming a Certified B Corp, along with a triple-bottom-line approach: people, planet, and profit. There are 86 such companies in Canada (including Left Coast Naturals).

> ## We're all connected and should be working together to educate, to empower, and to inspire to action.

As Manitoba Harvest continues to grow, Mike's willingness to fight the good fight shows no signs of waning. He knows what it's like to tackle potential roadblocks and to emerge from them a winner. He's keen that others are victorious too, and he's happy to coach them through the process in his role as healthy-food proponent, business owner, and recently, certified health coach.

"It's good to share our stories to bring inspiration to a lot of different people," he says. "I believe that anything is possible, and that's the best way to change society and the world. We can make anything happen."

199 *mike fata*

Hummus is a wonderful dip for fresh vegetables or pita bread.
It can be used as a filling for sandwiches, wraps, and rolls.

spicy hemp hummus

makes 4 cups

2 cloves garlic

3 cups canned chickpeas, rinsed and drained

1/2 cup hemp hearts (we prefer Manitoba Harvest brand)

1/4 cup hemp oil (we prefer Manitoba Harvest brand)

1/4 cup fresh lemon juice

2 tbsp fresh flat-leaf parsley leaves

2 tbsp ground cumin

1 tbsp red miso paste

1/2 tbsp freshly cracked black pepper

1 tsp cayenne pepper

1 In a blender or food processor fitted with the metal blade, combine all ingredients. Blend on low speed until smooth, stopping to scrape down the sides of the work bowl as necessary.

2 Transfer to a serving bowl to enjoy right away, or to an airtight container and refrigerate for up to 4 days.

A perfect sweet–salty combination, these granola bars are a delicious start to your day or a perfect snack. Make ahead and refrigerate for up to 1 week. Serve with fruit and yogurt or enjoy on their own.

hemp granola bars

makes 12 bars

½ cup liquid honey

½ cup packed brown sugar

3 cups granola

1 cup hemp hearts (we prefer Manitoba Harvest brand)

½ cup unsweetened dried cranberries

½ cup raw almonds

¼ cup raw pumpkin seeds

2 tsp kosher salt

½ tsp ground cinnamon

1 Preheat the oven to 175°F. Line a rimmed baking sheet with parchment paper.

2 In a saucepan over medium-low heat, combine honey and sugar. Heat, stirring occasionally, until sugar is melted.

3 Transfer mixture to a large bowl. Add granola, hemp hearts, cranberries, almonds, pumpkin seeds, salt, and cinnamon. Spread mixture in an even layer over the prepared baking sheet, using a rubber spatula to smooth the top. Bake in the preheated oven for 15 minutes, or until edges are lightly golden brown. Remove from the oven and let cool completely in the pan.

4 Using the parchment liner, lift baked granola onto a work surface. Cut into squares or bars as desired.

Recipe compliments of Chef Ben—a culinary friend of Manitoba Harvest.

Miriam Streiman

Chef & co-owner
· Mad Maple Country Inn ·
Creemore, ON

Hometown: Toronto, ON

It was the sheer joy of planting something and watching it grow in a vegetable garden that made Miriam Streiman truly fall in love with fresh-from-the-earth ingredients. In her eyes, the dirt under her fingernails and the bunch of muddy beets in her hands were, quite simply, beautiful. She decided that she wanted to ignite her passion for fresh food in others. But how?

After graduating from George Brown College in Toronto, the newly minted chef travelled worldwide, including to Japan, to quench her thirst for learning culinary traditions. But it was Miriam's time in Italy that shaped the course of her life. While there, she stayed in homes where meals were prepared using ingredients off the land, a.k.a. *agriturismo*. The concept of vacationing at a farmhouse, though commonplace in Italy, was less known in Canada. Miriam was determined to change that and help connect people with their food.

It took almost five years for Miriam and her husband, Neil, to find a place that ticked all the boxes for her own *agriturismo* business. "I thought that we'd get a place with one or two acres, perhaps," she recalls, "but when I was leading a farm tour with Slow Food at The New Farm, I was awed by Creemore's incredible beauty."

Miriam returned to the area shortly thereafter to follow her dream of living closer to where our food comes from. Upon seeing the 100-acre farm with its forest abundantly populated with maple trees and wild leeks, and the yellow-brick house circa 1890, she was smitten. That was the genesis of Mad Maple Country Inn, a place that would serve as an intimate classroom where Miriam could educate guests about the benefits of eating and cooking with sustainable, seasonal ingredients. After extensive renovations, the first guests were welcomed in 2012.

On a broader scale, Miriam continues to play an active role in the community. Beyond supporting the area's farmers and shining a spotlight on their work, she has helped pull together several food advocacy events, such as Soupstock/Foodstock, the Copper Kettle Cook Off (a Creemore event that raised funds for the local food bank), and Grow for The Stop (a fundraiser for The Stop in Toronto).

It's important to acknowledge that everyone should have access to good food.

Miriam helps spread the "good food matters" message by bringing producers, chefs, and the community together to learn from one another and support local food networks and the natural landscape. She also puts her renowned baking skills to work, donating goods, such as her popular maple red-fife scones, to the local food bank. "It's important to acknowledge that everyone should have access to good food," she says. "I feel a responsibility to my community and to use local producers."

Using her farm as a kind of culinary playground, Miriam takes pleasure in inspiring each of her guests to make real connections with what they eat, whether it's through cooking up a batch of maple syrup, churning butter, or foraging for wild ginger and chokecherries. She hopes it will help inspire change for this generation and the next. Maybe then she won't encounter children who have never seen a brown egg before, as was the case with one of her young visitors.

When she's not harvesting ingredients from the forest, planning community events, or leading workshops, Miriam is combing flea markets for vintage kitchen items. She has a slight obsession with rolling pins (seven and counting). "I feel the sense of history in them," she says. "I know that each has a story. I know they've been there when people have come together to eat and create memories. I find so much joy in that."

miriam streiman

This recipe is a tribute to the apples grown in Bruce, Grey, and Simcoe Counties. In addition to being a delicious dessert filling, it's perfect served with cheese or on toasted bread with a thick swoosh of butter. Or use it to sweeten other dishes. For best results, make it with homemade applesauce.

caramel apple butter

makes about 8 cups

2 cups granulated sugar

11 to 12 cups pure unsweetened applesauce

2 cups unsalted butter, softened

Pinch salt

1 Preheat the oven to 350°F.

2 In a wide, heavy-bottomed ovenproof saucepan over medium-high heat, heat sugar until it is completely dissolved and deep golden, 10 to 12 minutes.

3 Turn off heat and carefully whisk in applesauce (mixture will steam and splatter). Stir vigorously until completely incorporated, using a rubber spatula to scrape down the sides and bottom of the pan as necessary.

4 Add butter and salt and stir to combine. Bring caramel-apple mixture to a simmer over medium heat.

5 Place the pan in the preheated oven and cook mixture until reduced by half, about 2 hours, occasionally scraping down the sides of the pan to incorporate crispy caramelized sugar pieces and prevent edges from burning (see Tip).

6 Once mixture has thickened, remove from the oven and set aside to cool completely. Transfer to airtight jars and refrigerate for up to 2 months.

· tip ·

You'll need to be patient when cooking the Caramel Apple Butter in the oven. It may seem too thin, but it will thicken if you give it enough time.

We serve these delights as part of our bountiful breakfast at the inn—with a good cappuccino, of course. We love using Monforte Dairy's sheep's milk cream cheese in the pastry. Its rich tang perfectly complements the sugary flaky pastry and sweet caramelized apple goodness that oozes from the edges.

caramel apple butter rugelach

makes about 42

1 cup unsalted butter, room temperature

8 oz cream cheese, room temperature

1¼ cups granulated sugar, divided

¼ tsp sea salt

1 tsp vanilla bean paste or pure vanilla extract

2 cups pastry flour, plus extra for dusting

¼ cup packed brown sugar

3 tsp ground cinnamon

1 egg

2½ to 3 cups Caramel Apple Butter (see Tip, p. 210)

1 In a stand mixer fitted with the paddle attachment, or in a bowl using a wooden spoon, cream together butter and cream cheese.

2 Add ¾ cup granulated sugar, salt, and vanilla and mix until combined.

3 Reduce mixer speed to low and gradually add flour, mixing until just combined and a soft dough forms.

4 Turn dough out onto a lightly floured work surface. Using your hands, form a disc. Cover tightly with plastic wrap and refrigerate for a minimum of 1 hour or overnight.

5 Preheat the oven to 350°F. Line 2 baking sheets with parchment paper (you will need to bake rugelach in batches).

6 In a small bowl, combine remaining ½ cup granulated sugar, brown sugar, and cinnamon. In another small bowl, whisk egg to make an egg wash. Set aside.

7 Dust a clean, dry work surface with flour. Divide disc into four even portions. Roll one portion of dough out to a circle and spread caramel apple butter evenly over top.

continued…

8 Sprinkle some sugar mixture evenly over caramel apple butter.

9 Using a pizza cutter or a scalloped pasta roller, cut dough into wedges of your desired size. Starting at the wider edge, roll each wedge into a cylinder, ending with the tip. (At this point, rugelach can be frozen for baking later; see Tips). Place pieces on a prepared baking sheet. Repeat with remaining portions of dough.

10 Brush each piece with egg wash, and sprinkle generously with sugar mixture. One baking sheet at a time, bake cookies in the preheated oven for 12 to 25 minutes, rotating baking sheet halfway through cooking time, until golden.

11 Let cool on the baking sheet until filling has hardened. Serve.

· *tips* ·

To freeze rugelach, arrange unbaked rugelach in a single layer on a baking sheet and freeze until firm, then transfer to an airtight container. Rugelach can be frozen for up to 3 months.

If you don't have any Caramel Apple Butter on hand, you can substitute an equal amount of your favourite fruit preserve, blended until smooth.

Goodness is creating lasting smiles by sharing simple pleasures from the garden, like tasting a mint leaf, watching bees drink water, or teaching how to cultivate a carrot.

Esther Lily

Ned Bell

Chef
· Four Seasons Vancouver ·
Vancouver, BC

Hometown: Okanagan Valley, BC

You know how some chefs say that you've got to "walk the talk" to turn food philosophies into actions? Ned Bell took a different approach. He decided to cycle the talk as a champion for sustainable seafood. In the summer of 2014, Ned kicked off his Chefs for Oceans program by riding his bike from St. John's, Newfoundland, to Vancouver, BC, a journey that spanned more than 8,700 kilometres and 24 events over a 10-week period. The program was created to educate his peers about the importance of responsible aquaculture.

Ned's enthusiasm for seafood is entrenched in his DNA. He was born and raised on the West Coast. He grew up with fresh salmon and just-out-of-the-water scallops and mussels. Cooking in some of the best kitchens in Toronto, Calgary, and Vancouver, he became painfully aware that the all-you-can-eat-buffet we've been feasting on was headed for an abrupt end. Destructive aquaculture practices had to change—and soon.

"This is a discussion that chefs have been having among themselves for a while," says Ned. "We were aware of the problem, but there wasn't anything happening on a national level. It all came to a head for me in 2011 at the Canadian Chefs' Congress in Halifax. I realized then that sustainable seafood needed an advocate to build on the great work done by guys like chef Rob Clark, co-founder of the Vancouver Aquarium's Ocean Wise program."

Although his cross-country bike ride successfully sparked conversations about sustainable seafood, Ned realizes it was just the beginning. "There's so much work to be done. I'm trying to dispel myths, such as that seafood from

well-managed, responsible aquaculture is too expensive and not widely available. That's just not true. We've become addicted to cheap fish, and we need to rethink this, or else we won't have anything left in our oceans to eat. It's a resource that is not forever, and we need to protect it."

Ned is fine with standing on a mountaintop to preach to his peers, chef to chef, as well as to the public. He's out to educate us, and to shake us from our complacency. He points out that 2 billion people rely on the oceans for food and that, as Canadians, we are still importing two-thirds of our seafood from countries that put profit ahead of sustainability and even ahead of good taste.

Ned believes he has a responsibility to use his vocation to connect with people and effect change. He is out to prove that you can operate a seafood restaurant, be hyper-focused on sustainability, and still make money. He showed that with Yew, the Four Season Vancouver's popular—and profitable—eatery.

When he started his coast-to-coast journey by climbing onto his bike at the top of St. John's Signal Hill, accompanied by bagpipes, he was thinking about the long road ahead. He had left everything he loved—his wife, his kids, his job, his home. He even put up some of his own money to finance his journey. "I was prepared to risk it all to stand for something," he says. "I wanted to be able to tell my kids that I did something about food security—an issue that will affect their future. I wanted Chefs for Oceans to lead the way."

The happiest moment for Ned was the home stretch. While crossing the Lions Gate Bridge en route to the Vancouver Aquarium, he knew his family was waiting. "It was an incredible feeling. I had such a sense of accomplishment and pride, but I was also aware that the real work needed to start now."

True to his word, Ned has been pushing for March 18 to be recognized as National Sustainable Seafood Day, an opportunity to raise awareness of the need for healthy oceans, lakes, and rivers. With Ned championing the initiative, it's only a question of time before it too becomes a reality.

> *We have an obligation to educate each other in order to move attitudes around sustainability forward.*

ned bell

Fish tacos are spectacularly popular at Four Seasons Vancouver, and here I mix things up by using Pacific Dungeness crab, a sustainable seafood option. You will have lots of leftover vinaigrette—try it drizzled over grilled fish, roasted meats, or baked tofu.

dungeness crab tacos

serves 3 to 4

honey & lime vinaigrette

makes about 2½ cups

2 cups canola oil

2 tbsp golden miso paste

2 tbsp Dijon mustard

2 tbsp liquid honey or pure maple syrup

1 tbsp chili paste

Zest and juice of 2 to 3 limes

1 In a blender, combine vinaigrette ingredients and blend on high speed until smooth. Transfer to an airtight container. Vinaigrette will keep, refrigerated, for up to 1 week.

wonton taco shells

3 to 6 crispy wonton shells per person

1 To make taco shells from wonton wrappers, preheat oven to 400°F. Spray the inside and outside walls of a deep rectangular baking dish with nonstick cooking spray.

2 Drape the wonton wrappers over the dish's walls on the diagonal, forming triangular shaped "shells." Bake in the preheated oven until golden and crispy, 3 to 4 minutes. Remove from oven and let cool on pan. (Depending on how many people you are serving, you may need to do this in batches.)

continued…

taco fillings

1 lb ultra-fresh cooked
Dungeness crab

2 to 3 avocados, pitted,
peeled, and smashed

Juice from 1 lemon

Sea salt and freshly cracked
black pepper

1 In a bowl, combine 2 to 3 tbsp honey and lime vinaigrette (to taste, just enough to moisten the crab) and crab meat.

2 In another bowl, using a fork, mash avocados with lemon juice to desired consistency (chunky or smooth). Season with salt and pepper to taste.

assembly

1 radish, thinly shaved

¼ cup radish sprouts

1 Spoon mounds of mashed avocado on serving plates (just enough to set a taco on top of; see photo, page 215).

2 Fill or top crispy wontons so they are bursting with crab (about 1 heaping tbsp per crispy wonton). Garnish each taco with radish and sprouts. Arrange tacos on top of mounds of mashed avocado. Enjoy!

· tips ·

These tacos are also excellent made with an equal amount of Ocean Wise lobster.

You can also serve these with small soft corn tortillas or even butter lettuce leaves for wraps.

Goodness is a family
recipe that has been
passed down through
the generations and your
smile when you realize
that you will continue
that tradition with
your children.

Beth Dekoker

BC albacore tuna is the tastiest tuna because of all the beautiful oil in the fish loin—fat is flavour—and this preparation highlights it beautifully. While haskap berries can be difficult to find (they are a burgeoning crop in Nova Scotia; we got ours from Haskapa), the search is well worth it for their unique sweet taste. If you can't find any, you can substitute an equal amount of blueberries.

BC albacore tuna with "pickled" haskap berries

serves 4

"pickled" haskap berries

makes about 2 cups

3 cups frozen haskap berries, divided (see Tip)

3 tbsp birch syrup, maple syrup, or liquid honey

3 tbsp Venturi Schulze balsamic vinegar

1 shallot, thinly sliced into rings

½ tsp sea salt

1 Place 1 cup berries in a bowl and set aside to thaw, about 15 minutes.

2 In a small saucepan over medium heat, combine 2 cups frozen berries, birch syrup, balsamic vinegar, shallots, and salt. Bring to a boil, then reduce heat and simmer for 10 minutes, until thick enough to coat the back of a spoon.

3 Remove pan from heat and stir in reserved 1 cup thawed berries. Let cool.

· tip ·

This recipe makes more "pickles" than you will need for this dish. Store leftovers in an airtight container in the refrigerator for up to 2 weeks.

continued…

tuna

½ lb albacore tuna loin

Sea salt and freshly ground
black pepper

1 Season tuna with salt and pepper to taste.

2 Serve tuna raw or ultra-rare, cut into ¼-inch slices. (To serve ultra-rare, gently pan sear or grill loin for 5 seconds per side and then slice.)

assembly

Sea salt

½ cup hazelnuts, toasted
and crumbled (see Tips)

Camelina oil, for drizzling
(see Tips)

1 Place a piece of tuna on each serving plate. Season with salt.

2 Spoon 2 to 3 tbsp haskap berry "pickles" over each serving. Sprinkle with hazelnuts. Drizzle with camelina oil. Enjoy!

· tips ·

To toast hazelnuts, place in a dry skillet over medium heat and cook, stirring constantly for about 3 minutes, until lightly browned.

Camelina oil is a light, nutty-flavoured cold-pressed oil extracted from the Camelina sativa oilseed. It is rich in omega-3 and vitamin E. If you can't find any, you can substitute an equal amount of extra virgin olive oil, avocado oil, or hazelnut oil.

Goodness is not just a book about delicious good food—it's a way of life, as it should be for everyone.

Lisa Kates

Nick Saul

President & CEO
Community Food Centres Canada
Toronto, ON

Hometown: Toronto, ON

When he walks into his local coffee shop near the Community Food Centres Canada offices, Nick Saul is greeted like a visiting rock star. Everyone is excited to see him. And if you've ever met him, you understand why. He's a hugely charismatic guy with a clear vision of what needs to happen in order to secure good food for everyone. His passion is impossible to contain. It is passed on to others, from chefs to corporate leaders to volunteers, who in turn become ambassadors for change.

It might not have been clear early on in Nick's life that he was to become a leader in the fight against poverty, but the seed was there. Dad was a professor and anti-apartheid activist; mom, a schoolteacher deeply engaged in her community. But it was the family's move to Mozambique for a year when he was 15 that proved to be life-changing. He witnessed first-hand the harshness of life in East Africa. "I was born into a family that knew the world was bigger than their dining room table," he says.

In his final years of high school, Nick was more inter-ested in playing basketball than in politics, but his mem-ories of Africa lingered. As he furthered his education, he focused on social history—history from the bottom up. For his master's degree, Nick went to the Centre for the Study of Social History at Warwick University, later transferring to the Sociology Department. Upon returning to Toronto, he worked with homeless men in the city's east end.

"That caused me to ask, 'Why are people living in the Don Valley? Why can't we afford housing that's adequate and affordable for these guys?' Their lives

were disappearing in that valley. I knew I had to do work that was about justice, community organizing, and mobilizing people around policy change. Eventually I ended up at The Stop."

Back then, The Stop was just a food bank. Nick remembers thinking, "What is this? We're just handing out unhealthy food to people and sending them on their way. This is not okay." That's when the journey began. "I've said this often: it began by listening. It wasn't rocket science. It was simply an answer to the question, 'What does this community need to live a healthier existence?'"

Nick and his team then did an extreme makeover of the traditional food bank model. Gone were the line-ups for meals, the shame, the nameless participants, and the thinking that a hamper of processed, nutritionally bereft food was a one-size-fits-all answer to hunger. Instead, The Stop would be the catalyst for participants to become empowered—both individually and as a community—using food as a launching point for change. "We used to think about food as the end point, the goal in our anti-hunger work," he says. "Now we look at good healthy food as the beginning. A tool to bring about larger community change."

In 2012, Nick and a small team founded Community Food Centres Canada, a national organization dedicated to working with partners to create more Community Food Centres across Canada, as well as strengthen the broader food movement. It's a big job, and it takes someone who's equal parts stubborn, committed, and visionary to pull it off.

There's never really a time when Nick switches out of work mode entirely. His mind is always formulating plans. Even during a dinner out with his family—wife, author Andrea Curtis, and his two sons—he's thinking of the future. Andrea will ask him, "Nick, are you looking for the chef so you can ask him to help out at your next fundraiser?" He'll just smile. She already knows the answer.

> *You have to build organizations that reflect the future you want to see. Our organizations are about connection, dignity, health, and justice. They are expressions of where we can go.*

223 *nick saul*

This slaw is my take on one by Yotam Ottolenghi. It's tasty and packed with colourful root vegetables, it looks beautiful, you get to use a mandolin, and it's always worth the effort.

root vegetable slaw

serves 6

4 tbsp fresh lemon juice

4 tbsp extra-virgin olive oil

3 tbsp sherry vinegar

2 tsp superfine sugar

1 tsp sea salt

3 beets, trimmed and peeled

2 carrots, peeled

1 large parsnip, peeled

1/2 medium celery root, peeled

3/4 cup fresh cilantro leaves, coarsely chopped

3/4 cup fresh mint leaves, shredded

2/3 cup fresh flat-leaf parsley leaves, coarsely chopped

1/2 tbsp grated lemon zest

1 tsp freshly ground black pepper

1 In a saucepan over medium heat, combine lemon juice, oil, vinegar, sugar, and salt. Bring to a boil, reduce heat, and simmer, stirring frequently, until sugar and salt have completely dissolved, about 3 minutes. Remove from heat.

2 Fill a large bowl with ice water. Using a mandolin, cut beets, carrots, parsnip, and celery root into matchsticks. Place in prepared ice bath (this will help to retain their colour). Drain well, then place in a serving bowl and pour hot dressing overtop. Toss to coat well. Set aside to cool slightly. Cover and refrigerate for 1 hour.

3 Just before serving, add cilantro, mint, parsley, lemon zest, and pepper to marinated vegetables. Stir to combine.

4 Divide among serving plates. Enjoy.

Pots de crème always make me think of my birthplace, Dar es Salaam, Tanzania, and my parents and their commitment to social and economic justice. In our family, this dessert is served in small, beautiful ceramic coffee containers that coffee vendors used in the streets of Dar (shown in photo at left). Serve topped with whipped cream, if desired.

pots de crème

serves 4 to 6

1 package (6 oz) semisweet chocolate, roughly chopped

2 large eggs

1 tsp pure vanilla extract

Pinch sea salt

1 cup whole milk

1 Place chocolate, eggs, vanilla, and salt in a blender. Set aside.

2 In a saucepan, bring milk just to a boil, whisking constantly.

3 Immediately pour hot milk mixture over chocolate mixture. Cover and, using a kitchen towel, hold lid firmly (the hot liquid can cause the lid to pop off). Blend on low speed for 1½ minutes, until smooth.

4 Divide mixture evenly among ramekins. Refrigerate for at least 2 hours to set. Serve.

Paul Rogalski

Chef & co-owner
Rouge & Bistro Rouge
Calgary, AB

Hometown: Calgary, AB

Although he's travelled from California to Malaysia and points in between, it's Calgary, where he was born and raised, that chef Paul Rogalski calls home—and where he has operated his restaurant, Rouge, for the past 14 years.

Paul's the guy people know they can count on, whether it's to serve as a mentor to young cooking talents, to fundraise for charity, or to lend his voice in support of the quest for more responsible aquaculture and local sustainable farming. His breadth of culinary knowledge and generous spirit have made him and his restaurant an important part of the community. "It feels good to do what we can," says Paul. "What makes us happiest is making other people happy."

Paul understands the importance of building a strong community. In the fall of each year, he and his staff may participate in as many as eight events in a three-week period. "Community can be the four houses next to yours, or it can be the city you're in. No matter how you define it, every community benefits when you bring people together on common ground over food and the fundamental belief that nutrition is health. You see this at Community Food Centres where people learn about good food, work together, and begin dialogue on key issues. That's the key."

Restaurants for Change is just one fundraiser Rouge is involved in. Paul and his business partner, Olivier Reynaud, also organize their own fundraising events on behalf of the restaurant. Ride with Rouge is an annual three-day cycling event, held in July, that leads a tour through the Canadian Rockies to support Kids Cancer Care. And every fall they host the popular Rouge et Noir party in support of the Hotchkiss Brain Institute.

ROUGE
Restaurant
Paul Rogalski

When Paul isn't working at a fundraiser, he's likely either behind the stove or in his garden. He started his garden at Rouge when he opened the restaurant 14 years ago, before growing your own ingredients was the "in" thing in restaurant circles. He laughs when he remembers how diners back then shunned the dessert he offered—sauvignon ice wine with fresh raspberries, picked to order from the bushes just a 10-second walk from the kitchen. No one would order it. How times have changed …

It's good to give back. My staff and I are given great opportunities to contribute to our community and to be a part of truly amazing events. We want to be there.

These days, fresh produce like bright green herbs and perfectly plump tomatoes excite chef and customer alike—and, on occasion, a world-famous rock god. Paul had the privilege of taking Bruce Springsteen and his wife for a tour of his lovely garden. His garden is even home to two beehives, part of a program to boost the number of bees in the city. Paul describes the honey his hive produces as the best he has ever tasted.

You'd be correct to assume that Paul is fanatical about ingredients. He even makes his own butter and bacon. His passion was born out of an *aha* moment more than 20 years ago when he met John Ash, one of the pioneers of California cuisine. Paul literally blacked out after tasting a fresh fig, still warm from the sun, given to him by one of John's sous chefs. It wasn't the fig that sent him reeling—he chalks that up to anxiety and too many cigarettes (he quit smoking long ago). But just in that moment before he was out cold, he had a flashback to the times he spent at his grandparents' farm—and to the fresh foods and the flavours that were such a part of that experience.

"It was an epiphany," he says now. "It made me change my thinking about food being something to manipulate. Since then, I have treated food as it should be—something to be celebrated and cherished."

paul rogalski

My baba used to cook on the farm with a wood-fired stove and oven. She had the best garden and made everything from scratch. It was her epic meals that made me want to be a chef. To honour my grandmother's spirit, use freshly harvested ingredients and a wood-fired oven like she did. If those aren't options, a trip to the farmers' market and a regular oven will do, of course. Either way, roasting the vegetables is essential to creating flavour in this dish.

roasted cauliflower & parsnip soup

serves 8 to 10

4 medium parsnips, cut into small pieces

1 head cauliflower, cut into small pieces

1 medium yellow onion, roughly chopped

½ cup unsalted butter, cubed

1 tbsp chopped fresh thyme

2 cups dry white wine

10 cups chicken stock, divided

1 cup whipping (35%) cream

Sea salt and freshly ground black pepper

1 Preheat the oven to 400°F.

2 In a roasting pan, combine parsnips, cauliflower, onion, and butter. Place in the preheated oven and roast, stirring every few minutes, until vegetables are golden brown, 25 to 30 minutes.

3 Remove from the oven and stir in thyme and wine. Let stand for 5 to 10 minutes.

4 Transfer roasted vegetables and cooking juices to a blender and add 2½ cups chicken stock (you may need to do this in batches).

5 Blend on high speed until smooth (the hot contents can cause the lid to pop off, so be sure to hold it down tightly with a kitchen towel).

6 Transfer to a large pot over medium heat. Add remaining chicken stock. Bring to a boil, then reduce heat and simmer, stirring occasionally, for 5 minutes. Stir in cream and season with salt and pepper to taste. Serve.

When big beef flavour is on the docket, this is a classic. Serve with your favourite side dish, whether it be salad greens, a vegetable, or a starch, and enjoy with friends. This flank steak is also delicious served in a bun.

tangled beef flank
in sherry vinaigrette

serves 4 to 6

3 lb beef flank steak
(about 8 oz per serving)

¼ cup grainy mustard

¼ cup red wine

3 tbsp olive oil

1 tbsp fresh thyme leaves

1 tbsp fresh rosemary leaves

½ tsp chili flakes

½ tsp freshly cracked
black pepper

Sea salt and freshly ground
black pepper

1 batch Sherry Vinaigrette
(recipe follows)

1 Clean flank steak of any membrane and connective tissue.

2 In a resealable bag, combine mustard, red wine, oil, thyme, rosemary, chili flakes, and pepper. Add beef, seal bag, turn to coat well, and refrigerate for 2 to 3 days, making sure to turn meat occasionally.

3 Preheat the barbecue to 400°F.

4 Remove steak from marinade (discard marinade). Season with salt and pepper to taste. Grill for 3 to 5 minutes per side, covering with the lid to capture more smoke flavour, if desired (see Tip). Transfer to a plate and let rest for 10 minutes.

5 Using a sharp knife, carve flank steak across the grain into thin strips.

6 Toss beef strips in a bowl with sherry vinaigrette. Serve immediately.

· *tip* ·

Cook steak to desired doneness, but remember that more rare means more tender when it comes to flank steak.

continued…

sherry vinaigrette

1 tbsp Dijon mustard

3 tbsp liquid honey

⅓ cup canola oil

2 tbsp dry sherry

Sea salt and freshly ground black pepper

1 In a bowl, whisk together Dijon and honey. While whisking vigorously, slowly add oil. Whisk in sherry and season with salt and pepper to taste. Set aside until ready to use (refrigerate if not using immediately).

Goodness is a process
of becoming, not of being.
What we do over and
over again is what we
become in the end.

Joan Chittister

Paul Taylor

Executive director
Gordon Neighbourhood House
Vancouver, BC

Hometown: Toronto, ON

Paul Taylor grew up poor, raised by a single mom in downtown Toronto. For a large part of his childhood, they had no heat, no hot water, and no electricity. Food, when available, was something to rejoice and to cherish. His experiences early in life played a key role in shaping his views on poverty, social justice, and the importance of good food for all.

Paul studied political science at York University, then did an internship working with social justice activists at what was then called the Canadian Auto Workers union, which got him thinking about poverty's bigger picture. That led him to a pivotal realization: "We weren't poor because we were bad people, or because my mother had done something wrong. We were poor because there are systems in place designed to keep people poor. So that's when I said, 'I want to challenge those systems.'"

He had that opportunity when he left a job teaching at a private school to work at a homeless youth shelter. What Paul discovered on his first day horrified him. "The food that was served was tossed into the oven without any care, passion, or celebration," he explains. As the shelter's manager of food services, he ignited an interest in food among the youngsters by inviting them into the kitchen to cook with him. "We built on that momentum and started a catering operation, partnering with George Brown College to pilot an assistant cook's training program, a pre-apprenticeship program." It was clear evidence that food could be a catalyst for change.

Paul enjoyed his time at the youth shelter, but he wanted more. He wanted to delve deeper into communities to find out what was making them tick—and

causing situations where kids ended up in homeless shelters. In Vancouver, he joined the Downtown Eastside Neighbourhood House before making the transition to Gordon Neighbourhood House (GNH) in the city's West End, where one out of every three residents live in poverty. For decades, the facility had followed a long-standing charitable model for food banks that viewed providing food as the beginning and end solution to poverty.

Inspired by the good work of organizations like The Stop and other Community Food Centres, Paul was poised to shake things up. He said goodbye to the cafeteria-style lunches and introduced a chef excited to connect with those members of the community who came through the door. He launched urban farming sites that transformed unused green spaces into growing spaces and community herb gardens. And he's using his gifts for initiating conversations by addressing poverty as a systemic problem, participating in a poverty-education coalition and the Vancouver Food Policy Council, and pressing the provincial government to raise welfare rates. GNH is now one of 75 Good Food Organizations working in alliance with Community Food Centres Canada to offer health- and equity-based food programs in their communities. Through the program, GNH is able to access training, program tools, resources, and an annual conference where he's able to connect with other organizations across Canada doing similar work.

No one should have to live wondering where their next meal will come from or be marginalized for asking for help.

For Paul, pushing forward small initiatives is just as satisfying as pushing forward big ones. Whether it's the look of pride on the face of a boy who pulled out of the ground a carrot he helped grow or GNH abuzz with kids colouring and seniors having a cup of tea, for Paul, such victories are just as worthy of celebration.

237 *paul taylor*

This salad is an all-time favourite of mine. It's the perfect accompaniment for either lunch or dinner, or if you need to bring a dish to a potluck or dinner party. And you can easily make extra, since leftovers the next day are great too. The preparation is very forgiving. Be creative and play around with the ingredients to make it your own.

roasted potato salad

serves 4

6 to 8 red and yellow potatoes, cut into 1-inch cubes

4 tsp extra-virgin olive oil, plus more for drizzling

1/8 tsp each sea salt and freshly ground black pepper, plus more for finishing

1 cup diced cucumbers

1/2 cup diced dill pickles

1/4 cup each chopped fresh dill and green onions

2 tsp yellow mustard

2 tsp red wine vinegar

1 Preheat the oven to 425°F. Line a baking sheet with parchment paper.

2 In a large bowl, toss together potatoes, oil, salt, and pepper until well coated.

3 Arrange potatoes in a single layer on the prepared baking sheet and roast for 45 minutes, or until desired crispiness. Remove potatoes from the oven and let cool.

4 In a large bowl, combine cucumbers, pickles, dill, green onions, mustard, and vinegar.

5 Add cooled roasted potatoes and toss until well coated.

6 Season with a pinch of salt and pepper and a drizzle of extra-virgin olive oil. Serve.

Recipe courtesy chef Peter Nguyen, Gordon Neighbourhood House.

You'll need to get your hands a little messy to make this juicy chicken sandwich, but it makes for fun times in the kitchen. (It's a great way to get young people interested in cooking. I suggest finding a couple people who are willing to help.) I like to make this with chicken thighs, which are juicier and much more affordable than chicken breasts, but use whatever you have on hand. You can also serve on its own with your favourite side dish.

juicy chicken sandwich

serves 4 to 6

½ cup all-purpose or whole-wheat flour

2 large eggs

½ cup dry bread crumbs

⅛ tsp each salt and freshly ground black pepper

⅓ cup canola or vegetable oil

6 to 8 skinless, boneless chicken thighs

4 to 6 soft buns

Lemon wedges, for serving

1 Preheat the oven to 350°F. Line a baking sheet with parchment paper.

2 Prepare breading station: In a shallow bowl, place flour. In another shallow bowl, beat eggs. In a third shallow bowl, place bread crumbs and salt and pepper.

3 In a shallow frying pan over medium-high heat, heat oil until shimmery.

4 Meanwhile, working with 1 chicken thigh at a time, dredge chicken in flour until completely covered, then dip in egg wash, covering completely, and then cover thoroughly in bread crumbs.

5 Once oil is hot, working in batches, fry breaded chicken until golden brown, about 90 seconds per side.

6 Place fried chicken on the prepared baking sheet and bake in the preheated oven for 15 minutes, or until internal temperature reads 165°F on a meat thermometer.

7 Serve immediately on fresh buns with lemon wedges alongside and your favourite toppings.

Recipe courtesy chef Peter Nguyen, Gordon Neighbourhood House.

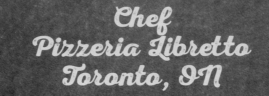

Rocco Agostino

Chef
• Pizzeria Libretto •
Toronto, ON

Hometown: Toronto, ON

The next time you're at Pizzeria Libretto, look for the smiling man near the kitchen. It's Rocco Agostino, a chef who finds joy in preparing good food and the contented grins that follow. It's not about ego strokes. It's about connecting—a big part of his life.

It's why his schedule is filled with charity events like Recipe for Change (on behalf of FoodShare, an organization that brings healthy eating to Torontonians), raising money for The Stop Community Food Centre, and lending support to initiatives around food issues. It's in his DNA to nurture and to embrace the people in his life as if they were family.

His Italian roots are in everything he does—including the Italian-inspired dinner he hosted for low-income families at the Christie Ossington Neighbourhood Centre in a Kids Cook to Care program. With two children of his own (ages six and three), he understands the importance and joys of teaching kids about good food.

His own attitude toward food was forged when he was a child. He remembers helping to prepare meals by picking tomatoes and cucumbers right off the vine in his family's garden. Using fresh, seasonal ingredients was the norm. He has taken what he learned about seasonality from his parents and applied it to his restaurant, which he opened in 2007.

That's why in winter customers won't find a traditional caprese salad on the menu. He opts to make his dish using locally grown beets instead—and it's a delicious thing of beauty.

As a chef and local-food supporter, Rocco's filled with fatherly pride when he sees his daughter sit down for a breakfast that includes freshly picked rapini, say, but he shares his appreciation for good, local, seasonal food outside his home and restaurant too—everywhere from chef-led events that benefit Community Food Centres to family pizza night at the Evergreen Brick Works. He enjoys watching kids pick tomatoes from the Brick Works garden and then incorporate their harvest in pizzas to bake. He is thrilled by the connections the kids make between good, local ingredients and good taste early in life.

Just as satisfying is seeing the change in people's everyday attitudes toward food. "People are becoming more educated and more passionate about what they are eating. I know the message is getting through because more customers are asking where the ingredients come from. They are becoming more accepting that ingredients are seasonal and may not be available all year round. That kind of knowledge is gratifying."

Rocco also believes it is important to sit down and eat with the people you love. "Everything happens around the table," he says. "Life itself happens. Big decisions are made, and it's the idea of sharing with people that is a big part of who I am. And when the food is good, that just makes the experience even better."

The most gratifying thing to me as a chef is not only giving customers a great experience but teaching people too. It's important to hand down knowledge. I am still working at learning as much as I can. I never want to become complacent.

If Rocco's dream came true, everyone would have a container or backyard garden. "It's a small way that we can all learn about good food," he says. "In that small way, we can all educate ourselves and let people know that we care about what we eat."

rocco agostino

A traditional caprese is a fresh tomato and mozzarella salad that is best served only when tomatoes are in season. During the rest of the year, we like to substitute locally sourced beets, which provide a delicious earthy sweetness.

· *beet caprese* ·

serves 4

4 beets, trimmed and scrubbed

½ cup white wine vinegar

Sea salt and freshly ground black pepper

½ cup White Balsamic Vinaigrette (recipe follows)

8 oz mozzarella, sliced into ¼-inch-thick rounds

6 fresh basil leaves, coarsely torn

3 tbsp extra-virgin olive oil

1 Place beets in a saucepan. Add vinegar and cover with water. Bring to a boil. Reduce heat and simmer until beets are tender (you should be able to pierce the beets easily with a knife), 15 to 20 minutes.

2 Drain beets and place in an ice bath until cool enough to handle.

3 Using your fingers (wear gloves, if desired, to prevent staining your hands), slip skins off beets (discard skins).

4 Slice beets into ¼-inch-thick rounds. Transfer to a bowl, season with salt and pepper to taste, add vinaigrette, and toss to coat well.

5 Place mozzarella in a separate bowl and season with salt and pepper to taste.

6 Arrange slices of beets and cheese in an alternating pattern on a serving tray. Garnish with ripped basil. Drizzle with oil. Serve immediately.

white balsamic vinaigrette

makes ¾ cup

¼ cup white balsamic vinegar

1 tsp liquid honey

½ cup extra-virgin olive oil

1 In a small bowl, whisk together vinegar and honey. While whisking vigorously, whisk in oil.

· *tip* ·

Store leftover vinaigrette in an airtight container in the refrigerator and enjoy drizzled on fresh salad greens.

Arancini are traditional Italian-style risotto balls. My mother used to make them on a regular basis as a savoury treat when I was younger. Her Sicilian arancini were quite large (about the size of a baseball), stuffed with meat sauce, cheese, and fresh peas. I've tweaked this recipe slightly to showcase the ooey-gooey mozzarella and made them a smaller size that is more appropriate for sharing with friends and loved ones.

arancini with mozzarella

serves 4 to 6

6 cups vegetable stock

¼ cup olive oil

1 medium onion, finely diced

¼ cup sea salt, divided

1 cup arborio rice

1 cup dry white wine

¼ cup butter

½ cup freshly grated Parmesan cheese

1 cup finely chopped fior di latte (mozzarella)

8 cups vegetable oil

4 cups dry bread crumbs

1 In a saucepan, bring stock to a low simmer.

2 In another saucepan over medium heat, heat oil. Add onion and 1½ tbsp salt and cook, stirring continuously, until onion is translucent (be careful not to colour the onion), about 4 minutes.

3 Add rice and sauté until edges are translucent (you will hear rice snap and crackle in the pan), 2 to 3 minutes.

4 Add wine and cook, stirring continuously, until rice has absorbed wine.

5 Add just enough hot vegetable stock to cover rice and cook, stirring continuously, until rice absorbs all of the liquid. Repeat process, adding 1 to 2 cups of stock at a time, until rice is creamy and al dente (tender to the bite), about 20 minutes. Remove pan from heat.

6 Stir in butter and Parmesan until incorporated and rice is creamy.

7 Spread rice mixture evenly over a baking sheet and let cool slightly before placing the rice (still on the sheet) in the refrigerator to cool completely, at least 2 hours.

continued…

8 Once rice mixture is completely cool, transfer to a large bowl. Using your hands, mix in mozzarella until evenly incorporated. Cover and refrigerate for 1 hour.

9 Using an ice-cream scoop, scoop out a portion of rice and roll between your hands to form a ball. Set ball aside on a baking sheet and repeat with remaining rice mixture.

10 In a deep-fryer or a large pot, preheat vegetable oil to 375°F.

11 In a shallow bowl, place bread crumbs. Roll each rice ball in bread crumbs until completely coated.

12 Working in batches so as not to crowd the deep-fryer, fry breaded balls until golden brown, 4 to 5 minutes. Place cooked arancini in a big serving bowl and season with salt to taste.

· *variation* ·

In step 8, substitute 1 cup shredded scamorza (smoked mozzarella) for the fior di latte, and add 1 cup puréed squash and 2 tbsp chopped fresh sage.

*Goodness comes
from the soul with
fresh, local ingredients,
love, and passion.*

Ted Reader

Sarah Harmer

Activist & musician
Kingston, ON

Hometown: Mount Nemo, ON

For Sarah Harmer, farmland is a precious thing. She grew up on a farm in Mount Nemo, in Burlington, Ontario, where her parents worked the land. Her grandparents were also farmers in Brussels, ON, and Erindale, ON. With generations of her family so deeply rooted in agriculture, it's not surprising that she has become a vocal supporter when it comes to protecting it.

When Sarah heard that the rich agricultural land where she was raised could be destroyed and the land turned into a below-water-table quarry, she felt compelled to step forward and lead the charge against the industrial proposal. She founded PERL (Protecting Escarpment Rural Land), an organization seeking support to block the opening of an 82-hectare limestone quarry smack-dab in the middle of the Niagara Escarpment, a UNESCO World Biosphere Reserve. The quarry would have a devastating effect on the habitat, home to endangered species of flora and fauna. It needed to be protected. Sarah served as

spokesperson and gathered friends like Great Big Sea and David Suzuki to help her to raise funds and awareness.

After an eight-year fight, the company backing the gravel pit was denied its application for construction. It was a huge victory for the environment and for the people of the Mount Nemo community, including her parents, who still live in the area. There were other, personal rewards too. The battle was a life-changing experience for Sarah. It allowed her to become plugged in to her community. "I got so much out of this," she says. "I connected with so many people who felt the way I did, and I also learned so much about how government works. That might sound boring to some people, but it was amazing and demystifying to see how decisions were made."

When Sarah isn't leading, she's supporting in ways both big and small. She has lent her name, her talent, and her determination to a variety of causes and events related to the environment and food issues. She was on hand at Food-stock, an outdoor public celebration of Ontario's bounty in solidarity with the movement to protest against a mega-quarry to be built in Ontario's Melancthon township. It too was slated to destroy prime farmland. "There was such a great energy to this event," she recalls. "Citizens coming together for a common goal … People brought their own cups and bowls. It had such a homemade quality."

> *Through my activism, I've learned that the world isn't run by someone out there. It's run by all of us.*

She travelled further afield, to Wolfville, Nova Scotia, to participate in and perform at the 2012 Canadian Chefs' Congress. Sarah was particularly interested in learning more about the issues around genetically modified alfalfa and how it affects farmers, and she had a chance to attend lectures on the subject. "It was a terrific event," she says. "I was happy to be surrounded by chefs. They are rock stars. I took a backseat to those guys and gals."

She has also been on the front lines at events like the Greenbelt Harvest Picnic and a recent concert for Pull Together, a coalition of First Nations and environmental groups opposed to the Northern Gateway pipeline in BC.

Sarah does what she can on a smaller scale too, whether it's performing at an outdoor rally for the National Farmers Union in Kingston, Ontario, or putting her money where her food is and purchasing baskets of fresh produce from the local CSA (community-supported agriculture). "It's just part of being an active citizen," she explains.

sarah harmer

I have difficulty finding tasty savoury vegetable pies, so this recipe,
adapted from *Salt Spring Island Cooking*, by Rodney Polden and Pamela Thornley,
is a personal favourite. It has it all: delicious veggies, savoury herbs, and
melty cheese surrounded by flaky melt-in-your-mouth pastry.

savoury veggie pie

makes two 8-inch pies

pie crust

3 cups whole-wheat pastry flour
(regular pastry flour works too)

1 cup cold butter, cut into pieces

1 tsp sea salt (optional)

⅔ cup cold water

1 Set aside two 8-inch pie plates.

2 In a food processor fitted with the pastry blade, combine flour, butter, and salt (if using).

3 With the motor running, add water and process just until a slightly wet dough forms (be careful not to over-mix or the pastry will be tough).

4 Turn dough out onto a lightly floured work surface. Pat into a disc and divide into 2 equal portions.

5 Using a lightly floured rolling pin, roll out each portion of dough to an 11-inch-diameter (approx.) circle.

6 Transfer each portion of dough to a pie plate by loosely rolling around the rolling pin. Centre the rolling pin over the pie plate, then gently unroll dough into the pie plate. Trim the edges, and prick bottom and sides with the tines of a fork. Cover with a kitchen towel and set aside until ready to use.

continued…

filling

3 tbsp olive oil

10 cups chopped cauliflower

2 cups chopped red and yellow bell peppers

1½ cups chopped leeks, white and green parts

5 tsp chili powder

4 tsp chopped fresh dill

2 tsp chopped fresh basil leaves

¼ tsp freshly ground black pepper

⅓ cup all-purpose flour

Pinch cayenne pepper

¼ cup tamari

⅔ cup water

2 to 4 cups shredded cheese of your choice

1 Preheat the oven to 350°F.

2 In a skillet over medium heat, heat oil. Add cauliflower, bell peppers, leeks, chili powder, dill, basil, and pepper and sauté until vegetables are softened, about 15 minutes.

3 In a small bowl, combine flour and cayenne. Sprinkle over vegetables and stir to coat well.

4 Stir in tamari and, if needed, water (if the vegetable mixture is already quite watery from the tamari, I often don't add any water) and cook until sauce thickens, about 5 minutes. Remove from heat.

5 Divide vegetable mixture evenly between the prepared pie shells.

6 Sprinkle 1 to 2 cups shredded cheese, to taste, overtop each pie.

7 Bake in the preheated oven for 30 to 40 minutes, until cheese is melted and bubbling and crust is golden brown. Remove from the oven and let cool for 5 minutes before serving.

· tip ·

Leftovers will keep for up to 5 days in an airtight container in the refrigerator.

*Goodness is when a
taste takes you back to
a place and time: eating
fresh fruit in a tiny
Okanagan kitchen,
drinking wine on a terrace
in Chianti with the air
heavy with sunshine
and rosemary...*

Twyla Campbell

This easy recipe has made a big squash lover out of me—it's also a great way to use up whatever veggies you have in your crisper. I usually make this with a mixture of chopped carrots, celery, and broccoli, but you can use whatever vegetables you have on hand.

squash pesto feta bake

serves 4 to 6

2 butternut or spaghetti squash, halved lengthwise, seeds removed

2 tbsp olive oil

3 cloves garlic, minced

1 onion, chopped

4 cups chopped vegetables (carrots, celery, broccoli)

2 to 3 tbsp basil pesto

1 cup crumbled feta cheese

1 cup dry bread crumbs (see Tip)

1 cup shredded cheddar cheese

· tip ·

You can make your own bread crumbs by toasting slices of bread on a baking sheet in a preheated 350°F oven for 10 to 15 minutes. Let cool, then tear into chunks and process in a food processor until fine.

1 Preheat the oven to 350°F. Lightly grease a large casserole dish.

2 Place squash cut side down in a baking pan. Add just enough water to cover bottom of the pan. Bake in the preheated oven for 40 minutes, or until fork-tender (make sure water doesn't completely evaporate while baking; keep an eye on it and add more water if needed).

3 Meanwhile, in a skillet over medium heat, heat oil. Add garlic and onion and cook, stirring occasionally, until softened, about 5 minutes. Stir in chopped vegetables. Remove from heat.

4 Scoop cooked squash into the prepared casserole dish, using the spoon to cut it into smaller chunks (discard skin). If squash is watery, spoon or pour out liquid. Add vegetable mixture and stir to combine. Add pesto to taste and feta and stir until evenly distributed.

5 Cover with a lid or aluminum foil and bake in the preheated oven for 30 minutes, or until vegetables are tender and mixture is piping hot.

6 Remove from the oven. Uncover and sprinkle with bread crumbs. Top with an even layer of shredded cheese. Broil on High, uncovered, for 5 to 10 minutes, until cheese is melted. Remove from the oven and let rest for 5 minutes before serving.

Scott MacNeil

Community chef
The Stop Community Food Centre
Toronto, ON

Hometown: Aurora, ON

For Scott MacNeil, his position as a community chef at The Stop in Toronto was the result of two worlds converging. After studying sociology at York University, Scott found a job in Hamilton helping people in precarious housing situations and trying to improve living conditions in rooming houses. As much as he found the work worthwhile, his lifelong dream of becoming a chef pulled him in a new direction. After attending culinary school at Niagara College and working in Niagara-on-the-Lake for a couple of years, he started working as a chef in Toronto.

It wasn't long before The Stop and its unique anti-poverty and anti-hunger initiatives got his attention. And it got him thinking. "I wanted there to be more to my cooking," he says, "a way to bring things together with the previous history I had with non-profits and working with vulnerable populations."

As luck would have it, the Community Food Centre had a vacancy for a chef. Knowing he would be a great fit, Scott was persistent in his pursuit of the opportunity—he was sure that The Stop was where he was meant to be.

Six years on, working at The Stop has been every bit as rewarding, challenging, and joyful as he imagined it would be. He has been able to play a part in its evolution and growth. "When I first started, we offered two lunches and two snacks a week and were more reliant on packaged food products," he recalls. "Now we are doing four breakfasts and five full lunches a week. 'Busy' back then meant feeding 90 people. On average, today, it's 150 and sometimes as many as 200. You can really see the impact that the economic crisis and government policies have had on the community."

Scott has also expanded The Stop's relationships with local suppliers, using heirloom, organic produce from The New Farm and organic poultry from Yorkshire Valley Farms and Bluegoose Pure Foods, to name just a couple. He uses healthy ingredients to bring nutritious meals and a variety of flavours to program participants—for example, Argentinean barbecue or vegetarian dishes from South India. "My mission is to provide food that speaks to everyone in a very diverse population," he says. "I want to provide meals that reflect our population. We make dishes inspired from all over the world."

In an effort to boost nutrition levels, he has become infamous for his ninja tactics using what he calls "secret kale." He chops it finely and adds it to soups, salads, wraps, and sandwich fillings. He knows that every bite counts, and that the meal someone enjoys might be the only one he or she has that day. He is also aware that quality food provides energy and helps tackle larger diet-related health problems such as diabetes and obesity. "People should not be grateful for just whatever they get," he says. "They have the right to receive good, healthy, quality food. It's a basic human right. We want to help perpetuate that in a big way."

Scott's job has its challenges—primarily, sustaining high-quality food levels within a budget—but those challenges are outweighed by the positive impact of the centre and of the meals he makes. "I've had someone tell me how happy she was that she put on weight after years of not being able to," he says. "And it's attributed to the food I make. I also get to see faces brighten after they've had something good to eat. And I get to make connections with people, like the woman I call my third grandma. She comes to see me every day to say hi. Or the former volunteer who was really struggling, then went off to cooking school. We've been able to create relationships with a lot of people and make a positive impact."

> *We serve healthy, whole food that is prepared with care at The Stop. No one has to line up. Participants sit down and they are served with dignity. That's one of our guiding philosophies.*

259 *scott macneil*

The first year The Stop started working with The New Farm in Creemore, Ontario, the farm supplied The Stop's food bank and drop-in with bushels and bushels of the most beautiful heirloom tomatoes you could ever imagine, in every variety. We really wanted to showcase the tomatoes in a way that preserved their simple awesomeness, so I developed this recipe, which is based on an Alsatian tart recipe. Serve with a simple arugula salad.

easiest summer tomato tart

makes 6 to 8 individual tarts

2 tbsp butter

3 leeks, white parts only, sliced

2 tbsp Dijon mustard

3 to 5 sprigs fresh oregano, leaves only

Salt and freshly ground black pepper

1 package (1 lb) frozen puff pastry

1 cup shredded Gruyère cheese

3 to 4 large tomatoes, sliced (1/2 inch thick)

Fresh basil, cut into chiffonade, for garnish

1 Preheat the oven to 375°F. Line a baking sheet with parchment paper.

2 In a large saucepan over medium-low heat, melt butter. Add leeks and sauté until softened, about 10 minutes. Stir in Dijon and oregano, and season with salt and pepper to taste. Remove from heat and let cool.

3 Roll out (or unroll) puff pastry to desired size and cut into 6 or 8 squares, as desired. Transfer to the prepared baking sheet. Lightly brush with egg wash. Using the tines of a fork, prick the centre of each square. Divide leek mixture evenly among squares, leaving a 1/2-inch border. Top with shredded cheese.

4 Arrange tomato slices in an overlapping concentric circle over the cheese. Sprinkle with salt and pepper and bake in the preheated oven for 40 minutes, until tomatoes look wrinkled and pastry is golden brown. Remove from the oven.

5 Sprinkle tarts with thinly sliced basil leaves. Serve immediately.

I like to welcome summer each year with a super-earthy plate of grilled goodness. To say that I adore burdock is an understatement. I love that it's the root of a nuisance plant, hated by most farmers; that it's totally unique in its flavour; and that it is quite strong medicine, rooting and grounding us.

grilled skirt steak *with* grilled asparagus & burdock root purée

serves 4

burdock root purée

2 cups milk (1% or 2%)

2 cups vegetable stock or water

Juice of 1 lemon, then lemon cut into slices

Sea salt and freshly ground black pepper

4 to 6 medium burdock roots

4 cloves garlic, lightly crushed

1 medium potato, peeled and diced

1 large onion, julienned

1/4 medium celery root, peeled and diced

Cold butter (optional)

1 In a heavy-bottomed pot, combine milk, stock, lemon juice, and lemon slices. Season with salt and pepper to taste.

2 Peel burdock roots and cut into 2- × 1/2-inch sticks (see Tip, page 264). After cutting each piece of burdock, immediately add to milk mixture to prevent it from discolouring. (Make sure burdock is completely covered in liquid; add more milk if necessary.)

3 Add garlic, potato, onion, and celery root and bring to a boil over medium-high heat (don't worry if milk separates). Reduce heat and simmer until vegetables are tender, 20 to 30 minutes.

4 Place a large bowl under a fine-mesh sieve and strain vegetables, reserving liquid but discarding lemon.

5 Transfer cooked vegetables to a food processor fitted with the metal blade. Add a few knobs of cold butter (if using) and purée, adding just enough reserved cooking liquid to achieve a thick, smooth consistency.

continued…

6 Using a rubber spatula, pass purée through a fine-mesh sieve into a saucepan, scraping the underside of the sieve (don't miss any of that delicious purée); discard solids. Add additional cooking liquid to saucepan if mixture appears too thick.

7 Gently heat purée until thickened slightly. Adjust seasoning to taste. Keep warm until ready to use.

· *tips* ·

As long as all the burdock root is cut to a similar size, it doesn't matter what shape you cut it.

The burdock purée is also delicious with grilled lamb or duck, fattier fish such as trout or salmon, and other earthy flavours such as mushrooms or roasted Jerusalem artichokes.

grilled skirt steak

¼ cup good-quality oil (canola, grapeseed, or olive)

5 sprigs fresh thyme, leaves only

5 cloves garlic, minced

1 to 2 lb skirt steak (or hanger or flank steak)

Sea salt and freshly ground black pepper

1 In a resealable bag, combine oil, thyme, and garlic. Add steak, seal bag, turn to coat well, and refrigerate for at least 4 hours or overnight. (Bring to room temperature and let rest for 1 hour before using.)

2 Preheat the barbecue or grill to high.

3 Remove meat from marinade (discard marinade) and let drain on a wire rack set over a baking sheet for 5 minutes. Season meat very heavily with salt and pepper.

4 Grill steaks once on each side until desired doneness. (I like to cook steaks until medium-rare: still soft to the touch, but with some resistance when pressed with your finger—4 to 6 minutes per side, depending on thickness.)

5 Remove steaks from the grill (leave heat on) and let rest for at least 5 minutes before cutting. Meanwhile, grill asparagus (recipe follows).

grilled asparagus

3 bunches asparagus
(about 32 pieces),
ends removed

3 tbsp olive oil

2 cloves garlic, minced

Salt and freshly ground
black pepper

1 In a large bowl, toss asparagus with oil and garlic. Season with salt and pepper to taste.

2 Grill over high heat until slightly charred and slightly bendable, about 5 minutes (be careful not to overcook).

assembly

Good-quality flaked sea salt

1 Slice steak across the grain into $1/2$-inch-thick slices.

2 On each serving plate, place a large dollop of warm burdock root purée, just off-centre. Beside purée, lay 7 to 8 grilled asparagus spears across each plate. Drape with slices of grilled steak. Sprinkle with sea salt. Serve immediately.

Sharon Hapton

Founder & CEO
Soup Sisters/Broth Brothers
Calgary, AB

Hometown: Calgary, AB

When faced with a milestone birthday, most people think about marking the occasion, perhaps with an epic party or an adventurous trip somewhere. Not Sharon Hapton. The Calgarian mother of two was thinking in a different direction for her 50th. "I thought I needed to reinvent myself, and create some greater meaning in who I was and what I did," she says. "I had just become an empty nester and wanted an opportunity that would get me charged up again."

As long as she could remember, she had been the type of person to show up on the doorsteps of friends and family members with a pot of soup, especially in a time of need. It was her way of showing she cared—a means of nurturing the people she loved through food. Why not do that on a larger scale?

Sharon set out to start a non-profit organization that would provide soup to people who were struggling and would benefit from nourishment and, equally important, provide a clear message saying that they were not forgotten. She would focus her efforts on women and children fleeing domestic abuse and family violence, as well as on youth transitioning from a life on the streets to mainstream society.

She named her organization Soup Sisters—two words that just popped into her head while taking a walk one day. They resonated with her on all fronts. On March 3, 2009 (also Sharon's birthday), a group of women came together to chop, to cook, and to laugh during the very first gathering for soup making. "This company was basically created from nothing, and now there are events, 100 percent driven by volunteers, in 22 cities.

They bring a lot of meaning to many people." Broth Brothers soon followed, after Sharon realized that men were also keen to get into the kitchen.

The concept behind Soup Sisters/Broth Brothers is simple. People sign up and pay a $55 participation fee to make soup at a cooking school or restaurant. Led by an instructor or chef, the group gets to work using the ingredients and recipes provided. All get a hearty meal of soup and salad, plus a glass of wine, in return, while the batches of delicious soup are readied for delivery. At a single event, enough soup is made to supply an emergency shelter for a month. With a total of 25,000 participants across Canada to date, that's a lot of nutritious soup made with a whole lot of love.

Sharon isn't close to being done with spreading what she calls "a hug in a bowl" (a term coined by chef Christine Cushing at the launch event of the Toronto Soup Sisters). She's hard at work creating Soup Siblings, an initiative that will get kids at the stove making soup for other youths.

"It's important to have this entry-level volunteer component. Kids learn not only about kitchen skills and nutrition but also how to work together. We make sure there is messaging at every event so they know where the food is going and they can make that connection to the people eating the soup they made."

Sharon is setting her sights on rolling out Soup Sisters across the United States (there is one location already in Los Angeles), and perhaps also Soup Sisters retail products, with 100 percent of the proceeds going back into the program. She is bursting with ideas. "I am obsessive with seeing each idea through," she says.

In the meantime, Sharon says, she is working harder than ever. She speaks regularly to volunteers across the country and personally attends all the launches for Soup Sisters programs. The hours she works are very long, but the rewards are plentiful. "We have provided over half a million servings of soup!" Sharon says with a smile.

> There is such goodness surrounding this. Every day is amazing. Every day is a highlight because warm and wonderful things just come your way.

This soup is my mother's recipe and remembered as a favourite when we were growing up. The simple ingredients combine to create great flavour. Our mother says she used cream from an elderly aunt who got it from nearby Hutterite farmers, and that it was so heavy it had to be spooned out of the jar! The soup makes a great base for all sorts of add-ins: frozen peas and corn, shrimp, or firm fish are all good.

potato leek soup

serves 5 to 6

¼ cup butter

3 large leeks, white parts only, thinly sliced

¼ cup all-purpose flour

7 cups water

7 medium Yukon Gold potatoes, peeled, halved, and thinly sliced

Salt and freshly ground black pepper

1 cup whipping or table (35% or 18%) cream

Finely chopped fresh flat-leaf parsley, for garnish (optional)

1 In a large pot over low heat, melt butter. Add leeks. Cook, covered, until leeks have softened, about 5 minutes.

2 Stir in flour. Cook, stirring, for 1 minute.

3 Gradually add water, stirring constantly to avoid lumps.

4 Add potatoes and salt and pepper to taste. Bring to a boil, stirring constantly.

5 Reduce heat and simmer, covered, until potatoes are tender, about 35 minutes.

6 Add cream. Simmer until heated through.

7 Ladle up steaming bowlfuls and scatter with parsley (if using). Bon appétit!

Our favourite mix of ancient grains and rice includes medium-grain red rice, Himalayan long-grain red rice, hull-less barley, black barley, rye berries, whole oats, and quinoa, but feel free to use your favourite mix, or come up with your own combo.

chicken creole *with* ancient grains

serves 5 to 6

2 tbsp vegetable oil

5 slices bacon, diced

3 skinless, boneless chicken breasts, diced

3 onions, diced

4 ribs celery, diced

1 green bell pepper, seeded and diced

3/4 cup ancient grains/rice mix (see headnote)

4 cloves garlic, minced

1 tsp dried thyme

1 tsp chili powder

2 bay leaves

8 cups chicken stock

1 can (28 oz) diced tomatoes, with juice

1 tsp Tabasco or other hot sauce

1 tsp Worcestershire sauce

Salt and freshly ground black pepper

1 Heat a large pot over medium heat. Add oil and bacon. Sauté bacon until crispy. Using a slotted spoon, transfer bacon to a plate lined with paper towel.

2 In the same pot over medium heat, add chicken, onions, celery and bell pepper and sauté until onions are softened.

3 Stir in ancient grains/rice mix, garlic, thyme, chili powder, and bay leaves. Add stock and tomatoes. Increase heat to high and bring mixture to a boil. Reduce heat to medium-low and simmer, uncovered, until grains are tender, about 35 minutes.

4 Discard bay leaves. Stir in Tabasco and Worcestershire sauces, and season with salt and pepper to taste.

5 Crumble cooled cooked bacon into bits.

6 Ladle up a hearty cup of chunky soup and garnish with bacon bits.

Todd Perrin

Executive chef & owner
Mallard Cottage
St. John's, NL

Hometown: Long Pond, Conception Bay South, NL

Todd Perrin is a proud Newfoundlander. He has a deep understanding of the need to create a strong community. The province where he was born and raised is legendary for its special brand of hospitality and warmth, extended to both locals and those "from away." Through his support of a long list of causes, Todd carries on the tradition in order to help create a good place to live—for everyone.

At the top of the list are events and non-profit organizations tied to food security. "It is a significant issue right here in Newfoundland," he says. "I try to make people aware of what's going on. We have a three-day supply of food on the island. If the ferry stops running, you will have empty supermarkets." Todd is a prolific user of social media to get his message out. "Today, tweeting can be your soapbox, so I take advantage of that," he says.

Todd is also a supporter of Chefs for Change, which hosts a four-night event bringing together in Toronto more than two dozen of Canada's top culinary talents. It was held in support of Community Food Centres Canada, an organization that advocates for access to good food. "Good food is such a basic commodity. It gives you a leg up to the rest of your life. If you are undernourished and wondering how you are going to feed yourself, you can't really live your life to the fullest. You should not have to be of a certain social status to be able to do that."

The quest for good food is linked to education as well. It's something Todd takes seriously. Through his restaurant, he actively engages his customers in discussions about where their food comes from. In the case of Mallard Cottage, 95 percent of it is sourced within 100 kilometres or so. Not surprisingly, sustainable fishing is a hot topic. Recognizing that a healthy fishing industry equals healthy communities, he shuns large fishing corporations, opting for fishers operating small and mid-sized boats.

The greatest reward for his goodness is the thanks he and his staff get from the organizations involved. "We come in and do the glamour stuff, and the volunteers do all the hard day-to-day work," Todd says. "The best is that thank-you hug or handshake. I'm only good at one thing and, if that helps someone to raise money or awareness, I am super happy to help. I'd be sad if the day ever came when I wasn't asked."

> *Everyone has a role to play in bettering their community, whether it's picking up a piece of trash off the street or volunteering at a soup kitchen or shelter.*

That day is not likely to come anytime soon. Todd has been an integral, and visible, part of his community ever since he competed in season one of *Top Chef Canada*. He didn't win, but Newfoundlanders didn't care. He was family. Locals were supportive when he bought Mallard Cottage, built sometime around 1820 to 1840, in Quidi Vidi village and turned it into a restaurant. When the cottage went up for sale, Todd jumped at the chance to own it: he had coveted it for more than a decade. "It all fell into place and this was my chance, my dream restaurant," he says. "It was serendipitous how it all happened."

Like many things in his life, Todd plunged in head first, turning the former antique store into what would become one of Canada's newest critically acclaimed eateries, now in its second year. True to his Newfoundland roots, Todd uses his success to enrich the lives of its residents, whether it's by supporting heritage preservation in St. John's or by speaking on behalf of the seal meat industry. He's modest about all he's accomplished: "I'm just happy to pull my weight and do my part," he says. "It takes everyone to move a community forward."

273
todd perrin

Here is the Mallard Cottage version of a basic household condiment found in everybody's refrigerator. This recipe shows just how easy it is to make a classic.

house ketchup

1 tbsp oil

1 onion

2 cloves garlic, minced

1 inch peeled fresh gingerroot, minced

2 whole cloves

1 tbsp ground coriander

¼ tsp dried chili flakes

¾ cup + 2 tbsp red wine vinegar

⅓ cup packed brown sugar

2 lb tomatoes, chopped

1 In a saucepan over medium heat, heat oil. Add onion, garlic, and ginger and cook until softened, 3 to 4 minutes.

2 Stir in cloves, coriander, and chili flakes and cook until fragrant, about 2 minutes.

3 Add vinegar, brown sugar, and tomatoes. Bring to a boil, reduce heat, and simmer for 2 hours. Remove from heat and let cool.

4 Transfer mixture to a food processor and process until smooth. Using the back of a ladle and a fine-mesh sieve (or a chinois, if you have one), strain purée into a clean saucepan.

5 Simmer over medium heat until desired consistency is reached. Let cool and transfer to airtight containers. Ketchup will keep in the refrigerator for up to 2 weeks.

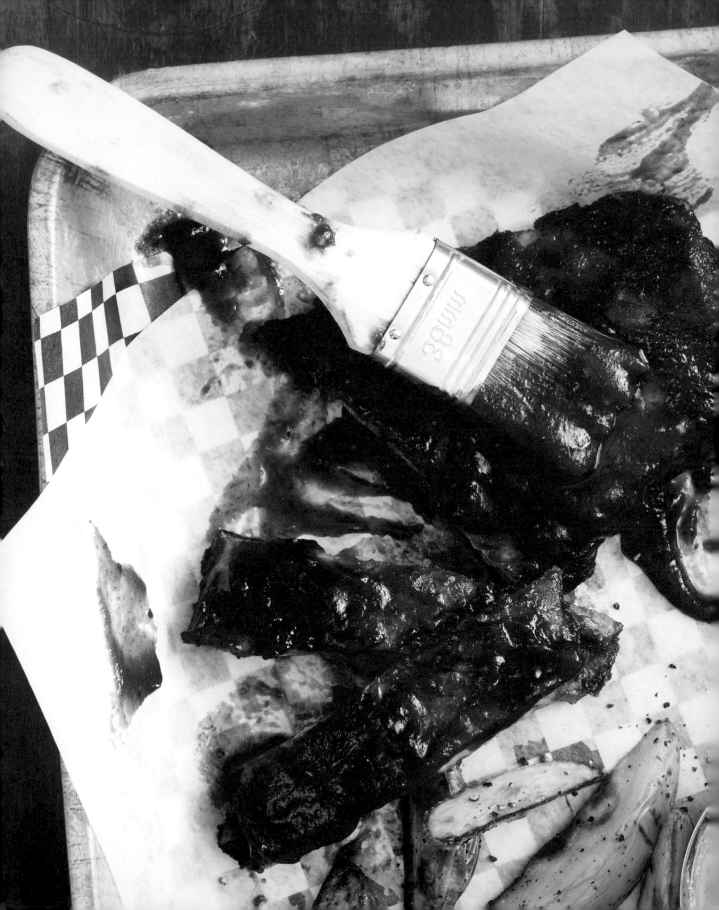

The addition of rum gives basic barbecue sauce some kick.
This is great on ribs, burgers, or even grilled salmon.

 rum BBQ sauce

makes 2 cups

1 small dried chili

¼ cup hot water

1 can (6 oz) tomato paste

1 cup packed light brown sugar

½ cup white rum

¼ cup fresh lime juice

1 tbsp minced garlic

1 tbsp fancy molasses

Kosher salt and freshly ground black pepper

1 Place chili and water in a small bowl. Let sit for about 30 minutes, until rehydrated.

2 In a medium saucepan over medium heat, combine tomato paste, brown sugar, rum, lime juice, garlic, and molasses. Stir well and bring to a gentle simmer.

3 Add rehydrated chili and soaking water. Season with salt and pepper to taste. Simmer until the flavours meld, 2 to 3 minutes. Remove from heat and let cool.

4 Transfer to a blender and blend on high speed until smooth. Transfer to airtight containers. BBQ sauce will keep in the refrigerator for up to 2 weeks.

A classic side dish, baked beans is a satisfying addition to any backyard barbecue or wintry Sunday brunch. It has a spicy-sweet flavour with a smoky tang, thanks to the addition of smoked onions (see Tip). This recipe makes a large batch, perfect for sharing.

baked beans

serves 16

6 cups dried white navy beans, soaked overnight and drained

1/2 lb bacon, diced

2 onions, smoked and chopped

3/4 cup molasses

3 cups tomato sauce

3 cups cider vinegar

2/3 cup packed brown sugar

2 tbsp sea salt

2 tbsp chipotle powder

1 1/2 tbsp chili powder

1 1/2 tbsp sweet paprika

1 tsp mustard powder

1 tsp freshly ground black pepper

1 Preheat the oven to 300°F.

2 In a Dutch oven, combine all ingredients. Stir well.

3 Add enough water to cover beans by 1 1/2 inches. Cover and bake in the preheated oven until tender, about 2 1/2 hours. Remove from oven and let cool slightly before serving.

tip

The easiest way to smoke onions is in a smoker (stovetop or outdoor) over medium-high heat. Quarter the onions and place in a pan. Cover tightly with foil, poke a few holes in the top, and smoke for about 1 hour, until soft and brown. If you don't have a smoker, you can use regular onions—the results will still be quite tasty!

Vikram Vij

Chef & co-owner
Vij's Restaurants
Vancouver, BC

Hometown: Amritsar, Punjab, IN

You can sum up Vikram Vij's philosophy in just four words: it takes a village. His approach to life revolves around being supportive of others because it's the right thing to do. It is evident in everything he does, whether it's promoting responsible aquaculture through the Ocean Wise sustainable seafood program, giving entrepreneurs a financial boost on CBC television's popular *Dragons' Den*, or making a generous donation to the University of British Columbia.

"Everyone at some point in life needs a helping hand," Vikram says. "Someone gave me a helping hand in 1994 when we opened our first restaurant. In the same way, it's time for us to give back to society and to fellow human beings who need help."

He would like others to have the same opportunities he has had to follow his dreams, so he's happy to be someone who can help provide them by taking a leadership role in his community and lending his star appeal to various events. "No one is forcing me to do this," Vikram says. "It's something you give from your heart. It feels good to share, to give, to discuss … I just feel like doing it, and I love it."

Vikram is known not only for his numerous accomplishments as a chef and businessman but also for his warmth, and he was recently awarded an honorary PhD from Simon Fraser University for bringing Indian food to the forefront in North America. Nothing pleases him more than to watch diners at his restaurants break into smiles after taking the first bite of one of his signature Indian dishes. He's big on making people feel welcome, as if they've received a personal invitation to come and hang out. This is a direct result of Vikram's you're-part-of-my-village-too spirit.

His drive to do good extends to his desire to share the food and culture of his native country. Few in Canada have done more to promote it. He calls himself India's "unofficial ambassador." It's a fitting title. Through his restaurants, his retail product line, and his philanthropy, Vikram has helped move Indian cuisine into the Canadian mainstream. He considers Indian cuisine a serious one, worthy of respect, right next to French and Italian. "It's more than just flavours," he explains. "It represents the diverse regions of India, its people and culture. And that's the key to understanding that Indian food is not just an ethnic food."

That was part of the reason Vikram donated $250,000 for extensive renovations of a culinary lab at the University of British Columbia. Students at the state-of-the-art facility, now called Vij's Kitchen, study food and nutrition, along with proper diet and its effects on communities. They also study the health benefits of various cuisines, including the medicinal properties of spices used in Indian cooking. "I wanted to do this because the community in Vancouver doesn't know what a great job UBC does with its program to do research and promote sustainable farming and seafood practices," he says. "It was important for me to highlight the invaluable work the university does and to encourage it."

When you take care of your village, your village will take care of you.

Vikram is also a strong supporter of his partner and co-owner of Vij's, Meeru Dhalwala, who he credits as a strong creative force behind the restaurants and a fervent supporter of Indian cuisine (she has written two extremely well-known Indian food "bibles"). Together, they have put their beliefs into action by supporting local growers. "Why would we bring in a frozen fish from India when there is beautiful sustainable fish right here in BC? Why wouldn't we help support someone local? There was never a thought that it was a cool idea, or a need to jump on the bandwagon. It just makes sense to want the best for your community."

Quinoa is an ancient and versatile grain that can be used in so many ways to create tasty and nutritious meals. This is a recipe I developed in 2014 for Plan Canada's Gifts of Hope quinoa project, and it's based on my experiences while travelling in Peru and India.

sautéed spinach & tomatoes with quinoa & paneer

serves 4 to 5

1 tbsp canola oil

2 tbsp chopped garlic

1½ cups chopped tomatoes

5 whole cloves (optional)

1 tbsp ground cumin

½ tbsp ground coriander

2 tsp sea salt

1 tsp ground turmeric

1 tsp cayenne pepper

1½ lb fresh spinach with stems
(about 3 bunches), chopped
into ½-inch pieces

10 oz paneer (see Tip)

2 cups cooked quinoa
(cooked in vegetable stock)

1 In a medium saucepan over medium heat, heat oil for 45 seconds. Add garlic and sauté until golden brown, 1 to 2 minutes.

2 Stir in tomatoes. Add cloves (if using), cumin, coriander, salt, turmeric, and cayenne and sauté until glistening with oil, 3 to 4 minutes.

3 Stir in spinach, paneer, and cooked quinoa and cook until spinach wilts and mixture has a saucy consistency (the paneer may start to crumble; this is normal). Cover and cook for 2 to 3 minutes, until piping hot. Serve immediately.

· tip ·

Paneer is a type of fresh (unripened) cheese popular in Indian cuisine. It has a milky flavour and dense texture. Because it doesn't melt like other cheeses, it holds its shape well when added to hot dishes. You can find paneer in well-stocked supermarkets or Indian grocers.

This is a signature family dish that I created for my daughters. One night while at a local restaurant, the girls wanted to order chicken nuggets while my wife, Meeru, was trying to get them to try something else. The next evening, I decided to show the girls what "real" chicken nuggets are: chicken schnitzel! And when my daughter Nanaki joked, "Hey, let's make butter chicken schnitzel!," I made the sauce on the spot.

butter chicken schnitzel

serves 6

homestyle butter sauce

¼ cup canola oil

2 to 3 tbsp crushed garlic (6 to 9 medium cloves)

1 small can (6 oz) tomato paste or ¾ cup crushed canned tomatoes, with juice

1 tbsp sweet paprika

2 tsp garam masala (optional)

1½ tsp sea salt

1 tsp ground turmeric

1 tsp ground cumin (or 1 tbsp if not using garam masala)

1 tsp ground coriander

1 tsp cayenne pepper (optional)

1½ cups water

1½ cups whipping (35%) cream

1 In a medium saucepan over medium heat, heat oil for 1 minute. Add garlic and sauté until golden, about 1 minute (it will become slightly sticky, but keep stirring). Add tomato paste and stir well. Reduce heat to low and add paprika, garam masala (if using), salt, turmeric, cumin, coriander, and cayenne (if using). Stir well and sauté for 4 minutes. Stir in water and cream, then remove mixture from heat and set aside until ready to reheat for serving.

continued…

chicken schnitzel

2 lb skinless, boneless chicken breasts or thighs, cut in 2- x 3-inch pieces

1/2 cup all-purpose flour

1 tsp sea salt

2 eggs

1 cup fine dry bread crumbs

1/2 to 3/4 cup oil, divided

1 Place chicken pieces on a clean work surface and lightly pound them with the heel of your hand to flatten to 1/2 inch thick. Transfer to a plate and set aside.

2 Spread flour on a plate and stir in salt. Beat eggs in a large bowl. Spread bread crumbs on another plate. Set aside 2 baking sheets: one lined with paper towel, the other not.

3 Working with 1 piece of chicken at a time, dip chicken in flour, lightly coating both sides. Shake off any excess flour, then dip chicken into beaten eggs, lightly coating both sides. Finally, dredge chicken in bread crumbs, making sure to coat both sides and to shake off any excess. Place coated chicken on unlined baking sheet.

4 Heat 2 tbsp oil in a deep-sided skillet over medium-high for 3 to 4 minutes, until oil is hot enough that chicken will start to cook immediately. (If the oil isn't hot enough, it will soak into the bread crumbs and you will have greasy rather than crispy chicken.)

5 Using a pair of tongs, add each piece of chicken (as many as will easily fit in the pan), then pan-fry each side for 3 minutes. Use a knife to cut into the first cooked piece: the meat should be white without any pink, and the flesh should be succulent, not dry. (If bread crumbs begin to burn within 1 minute, reduce heat. If oil is not sizzling around chicken, increase heat.) Transfer cooked schnitzel to the prepared baking sheet to drain. Repeat with remaining pieces of chicken.

6 Once all (or most) of chicken has been fried, warm prepared butter sauce on medium-high heat. As soon as it comes to a boil, stir well and reduce heat to low. Simmer for 5 minutes, then turn off heat.

7 Serve schnitzel with a bowl of butter sauce for dipping.

Slightly adapted from *Vij's at Home: Relax, Honey* by Meeru Dhalwala and Vikram Vij (Douglas & McIntyre, 2010). Reprinted by permission of the author.

Goodness is a leap of faith based on a smile and a feeling, and a hand extended without judgment or condition.

Tracy Bordian

where to find the goodness

Andrea Carlson
Burdock & Co.
burdockandco.com

Jenn Prager
Dartmouth North CFC
dartmouthfamilycentre.ca

Ashrafi Ahmed
Regent Park CFC
cfccanada.ca/regent-park-cfc

John Lai
Drake Devonshire
drakedevonshire.ca

Bertrand Alépée
The Tempered Chef,
thetemperedchef.com

Joshna Maharaj
Ryerson University
food.ryerson.ca

Brad Long
Cafe Belong
cafebelong.ca

Judy Dempsey
The Table CFC
thetablecfc.org

Carl Heinrich
Richmond Station
richmondstation.ca

Judy Servay
Robin des Bois
robindesbois.ca

Chris Brown
Citizen Catering
citizencatering.com

Keith Froggett
Scaramouche
scaramoucherestaurant.com

Elana Rosenfeld
Kicking Horse Coffee
kickinghorsecoffee.com

Kim Fox
NDG Food Depot
depotndg.org

Gillian Flies
The New Farm
thenewfarm.ca

Kristina McMillan
NorWest Co-op CFC
norwestcoop.ca/community-food-centre

Ian Walker
Left Coast Naturals
leftcoastnaturals.com

Lil MacPherson
The Wooden Monkey
thewoodenmonkey.ca

Jamie Kennedy
Jamie Kennedy Kitchens
jamiekennedy.ca

Lora Kirk
Ruby WatchCo.
rubywatchco.ca

Jean-François Archambault
La Tablée des Chefs
tableedeschefs.org

Michael Ableman
Salt Spring Island, BC
fieldsofplenty.com

Mike Fata
Manitoba Harvest Hemp Foods
manitobaharvest.com

Miriam Streiman
Mad Maple Country Inn
madmaple.ca

Ned Bell
Chefs for Oceans
chefsforoceans.com
Four Seasons Vancouver
fourseasons.com/Vancouver

Nick Saul
Community Food Centres Canada
cfccanada.ca

Paul Rogalski
Rouge & Bistro Rouge
rougecalgary.com
bistrorougeyyc.com

Paul Taylor
Gordon Neighbourhood House
gordonhouse.org

Peter & Chris Neal
Neal Brothers Foods
nealbrothersfoods.com

Rocco Agostino
Pizzeria Libretto
pizzerialibretto.com

Sarah Harmer
sarahharmer.com

Scott MacNeil
The Stop CFC
cfccanada.ca/the_stop_community_
    food_centre

Sharon Hapton
Soup Sisters/Broth Brothers
soupsisters.org

Todd Perrin
Mallard Cottage
mallardcottage.ca

Vikram Vij
Vij's Restaurants
vijs.ca

community food centres

Community Food Centres Canada
cfccanada.ca

**The Stop Community Food Centre,
Toronto, ON**
cfccanada.ca/the_stop_community_
    food_centre

**Regent Park Community Food Centre,
Toronto, ON**
cfccanada.ca/regent-park-cfc

**The Local Community Food Centre,
Stratford, ON**
thelocalcfc.org

The Table Community Food Centre, Perth, ON
thetablecfc.org

NDG Food Depot, Montreal, QC
depotndg.org

Dartmouth North CFC, Dartmouth, NS
dartmouthfamilycentre.ca

NorWest Co-op CFC, Winnipeg, MB
norwestcoop.ca/community-food-centre

**Gordon Neighbourhood House,
    Vancouver, BC**
gordonhouse.org

acknowledgements

As we quickly learned, putting together a project of this magnitude is not easy and requires talents and skills that we Neal Brothers don't necessarily have in our wheelhouse. We offer our heartfelt thanks to the following people who helped to make *Goodness* a reality.

The most important decision we made was to work with Tracy "The Contractor" Bordian, who embraced our concept from the very beginning. We wanted to work with people who understood what we were trying to accomplish, and Tracy guided us along this journey and ensured that the right people were involved (many of whom we are about to acknowledge). Tracy kept us on schedule and ensured that the book stayed true to its singular message: Goodness. Her involvement went far beyond what we believe a traditional editor's job entails, and for that we are eternally grateful. Tracy embodies Goodness to her very core. Not only did we hire an exceptional editor, but we have also made a lifelong friend!

Kyle "The Style" Gell designed and laid out our book and corrected copy as needed. He created an enticing cover that told our story, and then carried the look and feel right through, from the front cover to the interior pages to the back cover, and he nailed it!

Jodi Pudge, Noah Witenoff, Catherine Doherty, and their teams captured the beauty of our contributors' ideas of Goodness. The photos of the finished recipes (some half-eaten, which we love!) brought the combinations of ingredients to life and showed us what they could and should look like.

What truly separates our book from other, more traditional cookbooks is the stories of the people who have made wonderful contributions—and brought real Goodness—to their communities. Michele Sponagle's task was not easy, but she accomplished it beautifully.

Korey Kealey, special thanks for encouraging us to tackle a book in the first place.

Lisa Kates, thank you for your early support and contributions.

Nick Saul and Christina Palassio at Community Food Centres Canada, thank you for your support and help unearthing some great contributors, and for working tirelessly (often without gratitude) toward a much bigger goal. We applaud you. Your vision and commitment to nothing but the best for your organization should be heralded, and we hope that this project can help contribute to your work.

Goodness—the book—would not exist without the stories and work of the contributing artists, chefs, activists, and entrepreneurs who accepted our invitation to be part of this project. We thank you not only for the recipes and the interviews but, most importantly, for choosing to live and work in ways that define Goodness.

To our staff at Neal Brothers, we send a giant hug to all of you for supporting our vision and for your enthusiasm around this project.

As the saying goes, last but certainly not least, we would like to thank our families. To our parents, Mary and Stan, for setting the bar high and whose own lifelong community involvement has helped to nurture our values and the guidelines by which we choose to live our lives. To our wives, Wendy and Lara, and children, Sarah and Zoë, and Hannah, Rebecca, and Bridget, you continue to inspire us to make the world a better place for you.

credits

We would like to express our heartfelt thanks to the contributors for supplying their recipes and profile photographs, and to Renée Suen for contributing to our photo collage. Recipes and photos remain the copyright of the respective contributors and photographers, as specified here and on individual recipes.

Collage: © Peter & Chris Neal, with the exception of photos contributed by Renée Suen, Tracy Bordian, and Kyle Gell

Recipe photos: © Peter & Chris Neal, 2015. Photography by Jodi Pudge

Cutting boards for quotations: iStock.com/Lisovskaya, iStock.com/edenexposed, iStock.com/barol16

p. xx: iStock.com/grafvision

p. 2: Photo of Peter & Chris Neal at table © Lisa Kates; used by permission

pp. 10–13: Community dinner © Terri Manzo; Neighbours preparing a meal together © Terri Manzo; The Stop Community Food Centre's gardening programs © Zoe Alexopoulos; Kids pick herbs © David Zimmerly; Peer advocates © CFCC; NorWest Co-op Community Food Centre's Filipino Family Cooking Group © CFCC

pp. 14–15: © Zoe Alexopoulos

p. 16: Andrea Carlson—© Alison Page

index

a

Ableman, Michael, 192–93
Action Against Hunger, 147
After School Smoothie Drop-In, 160–61
Agostino, Rocco, 242–43
Ahmed, Ashrafi, 30–31
Alépée, Bertrand, 42–43, 68
Amuse-Bouche, 42
Anderson, Liz, 176–77
apples
    applesauce and caramel butter, 206
Archambault, Jean-François, 106–7
Ash, John, 229
asparagus, grilled, 265
avocados
    cream, 158
    green goddess dressing, 186
    guacamole, 108

b

bacon
    rösti, with cheesy scrambled eggs, 103–4
baked goods
    blueberry buckle cake, 94
    caramel apple butter rugelach, 209–10
    chocolate cake, 97
    ginger stout cake, 189–90
    gluten-free brownies, 181
    hemp granola bars, 203
    Kicking Horse Café's gluten-free cookies, 81
    leek and oatmeal biscuits, 57
    Rocky Mountain scones, 78
Banff Mountain Film and Book Festival, 77
barley
    risotto, 174

bars
hemp granola, 203
beans, baked, 278
beef
braised shank, 65–66
flank in sherry vinaigrette, 233–34
grilled skirt steak, 263–65
beet greens
sautéed, 89
beets
caprese, 244
roasted, 90
roasted, gouda, and pickled onion
salad, 168–70
root vegetable slaw, 224
Bell, Ned, 212–13
Bell Centre, 107
bell peppers
smoky chakchouka, 154
berbere spice mix, 144
berries
haskap, pickled, 219
biscuits
leek and oatmeal, 57
Rocky Mountain scones, 78
Bistro Rouge, 228–29
black beans
burrito bowl, 157–59
sweet and spicy mixture, 157
blueberries
buckle cake, 94
Boulud, Daniel, 58
Bower, Christine, 167
breads
homemade croutons, 111
breakfast
Don Valley pudding, 54
broths
sour bran, 21–22
Brown, Chris, 42, 68–69

brownies
gluten-free, 181
buffalo ribs
braised with red pepper pesto, 29
Burdock & Co., 16
burdock root purée, 263–64
burrito bowl, 157–59
butters
caramel apple, 206

c

cabbage
spicy slaw, 158
Cafe Belong, 52–53
cakes
blueberry buckle, 94
chocolate, with hippie flakes, 97
ginger stout, 189–90
Campaign 226, 177
Canadian Chefs' Congress, 212, 251
Canadian Foundation for AIDS
Research, 147
caramel
coffee, 190
caramel millefeuille
with pears and crème anglaise,
49–51
Carlson, Andrea, 16–17
carrots
maple-glazed, 86
roasted, 46
root vegetable slaw, 224
cauliflower
and kale gratin, 126
and parsnip soup, 230
celery root
purée, 65–67
root vegetable slaw, 224

winter root mash, 197
Centre for Arts, Ecology, and
    Agriculture, 192
Centre for Studies in Food Security
    (Ryerson University), 153
chakchouka, 154
cheese
    cauliflower and kale gratin, 126
    Don Valley Pudding, 54
    fondue, 178
    gouda, roasted beet, and pickled
        onion salad, 168–70
    macaroni and, 117
    scrambled eggs and bacon rösti,
        103–4
    squash pesto feta bake, 257
Chefs for Change, 69, 272
Chefs for Oceans, 212, 213
Chefs' Table Society of BC, 16
chicken
    Creole, 271
    Malaysian chicken, 123
    and quinoa salad, 129
    sandwich, 241
    schnitzel, 285–86
chickpeas
    and pancetta soup, 132
    spicy hemp hummus, 200
Child, Julia, 17, 147
chocolate
    gluten-free brownies, 181
    pots de crème, 227
Citizen Catering, 68–69
City Farm School, 153
Claiborne, Craig, 17
clams
    seafood chowder, 26
Clark, Rob, 212
coffee
    caramel, 190

kick ass french-press coffee, 82
Community Food Centres Canada,
    31, 42, 59, 69, 112, 130, 160, 161,
    176–77, 182, 222–23, 237, 272
cookies
    Kicking Horse Café's gluten-free,
        81
Copper Kettle Cook Off, 205
corn
    Don Valley pudding, 54
cornmeal. See polenta
crab
    tacos, 214–16
Crawford, Lynn, 1, 183
crème anglaise, 51
Cross Town Kitchens, 42–43, 68
croutons, homemade, 111
CSA (community-supported
    agriculture), 16, 84, 113, 251
cucumbers
    bread and butter pickles, 70
Cultivate Canada, 193
curries
    Malaysian chicken, 123
    shrimp, 35
    vegetable rainbow, 32
Curtis, Andrea, 223
Cushing, Christine, 267
custard
    crème anglaise, 51

d

dahl soup, 138–40
Dandelion Eatery, 36
Dartmouth Family Centre, 112–13
Dartmouth North Community Food
    Centre, 112–13
DB Bistro Moderne, 58

De Luca's, 165
Dempsey, Judy, 130–31
desserts
   panna cotta, 151
   poached pears in red wine, 165
   pots de crème, 227
   salted caramel millefeuille, pears
     and crème anglaise, 49–51
Dhalwala, Meeru, 280
Dirt Series—Mountain Bike Camps,
   77
Dish, 124
Diversity Food Services (University
   of Winnipeg), 36–37
Donovan, Ryan, 58
Dorland, Jason, 93
Downtown Eastside Neighbourhood
   House, 237
Dragons' Den (TV show), 280
Drake Devonshire, 119
dressings, salad
   apple cider vinaigrette, 170
   Brown Derby vinaigrette, 187
   green goddess dressing, 186
   honey and lime vinaigrette, 214
   sherry vinaigrette, 244
   white balsamic vinaigrette, 244
Ducasse, Alain, 43, 147
duck
   breast, with truffle jus, 44–46

e

eggs
   cheesy scrambled, 103–4
   crispy, and pork belly salad,
     184–87
   Don Valley pudding, 54
   orange meringue, 190

   smoky chakchouka, 154
enchilada pie, 9
Evergreen Brick Works, 52, 243

f

Fallah, Farzam, 59
Farm, Arts and Culinary Camp for
   Kids, 192
Fata, Mike, 198–99
Filipino Family Cooking Group,
   160
First Nations cuisine, 16–17
fish
   albacore tuna with haskap berries,
     219–20
   baked pickerel with mango salsa,
     162
   halibut crunch, 6
   marinated wild sockeye salmon,
     100
   salmon rillettes, 111
   seafood chowder, 26
   trout bourguignon, 60
Flies, Gillian, 84–85
Food Matters Manitoba, 160
food-recovery program, 106–7
FoodShare, 43, 242
Foodstock, 205
Four Seasons Vancouver, 212–13
Fox, Kim, 152–53
Foxglove Farm, 192
Froggett, Keith, 146–47

g

Gass, Matthew, 167
George, Andrew, 24–25

George Brown College, 52, 69, 118, 124, 204, 236
Georgetown Hospital, 147
gluten-free
  brownies, 181
  cookies, 81
gnocchi
  wild mushroom and stinging nettle, 73–74
Godbout, Kirsten, 37
Gold Medal Plates, 147
Gordon Neighbourhood House, 236–37
Gore, Al, 166
grains
  chicken Creole, 271
granola
  hemp bars, 203
Granville Island Market, 93
Great Big Sea, 250
Greenbelt Harvest Picnic, 251
Grow for The Stop, 85, 205
Growing Chefs! Chefs for Children's Urban Agriculture, 16
guacamole, 108

h

halibut
  crunch, 6
Hapton, Sharon, 266–67
Harmer, Sarah, 250–51
Harvest Community Foods, 16
haskap berries, pickled, 219
hazelnuts
  with mixed greens, 18
Heinrich, Carl, 58–59
hemp hearts
  granola bars, 203

spicy hummus, 200
Hospital for Sick Children, 125
Hotchkiss Brain Institute, 228
hummus
  spicy hemp, 200
Hungry Planet, The, 130

i

Inn at Manitou, 43
Institut de tourisme et d'hôtellerie du Québec, 106
Institut Valet, 43

j

Jerusalem artichokes
  winter root mash, 197
Johnson, Leo, 76
Jump, Jiggle, and Jive, 112

k

kale
  and cauliflower gratin, 126
Kennedy, Jamie, 98–99, 146
ketchup, 274
Kicking Horse Coffee, 76–77
Kids Cancer Care, 228
Kids Cook to Care, 242
Kirk, Lora, 182–83
Kla-how-eya Aboriginal Centre, 24
Kramer, Ben, 36–37

l

Lai, John, 118–19
lamb
    braised shanks with barley
        risotto, 173–74
La Tablée des Chefs, 106–7
Le Bistro de l'Etoile, 43
leeks
    and oatmeal biscuits, 57
    and potato soup, 268
    wild, and morel quiche, 148
Left Coast Naturals, 92–93, 199
lentils
    dahl soup, 138–40
    mujaddara, 143–44
lime oil, 140
Local Community Food Centre,
    176–77
Long, Brad, 52–53
Love Food Give Food, 147
Loving Spoonfuls, 177
Le Byblos des Neigres, 43

m

macaroni and cheese, 117
MacNeil, Scott, 258–59
MacPherson, Lil, 166–67
Mad Maple Country Inn, 204–5
Maharaj, Joshna, 124–25
Mallard Cottage, 272–73
mangoes
    salsa, 162
Manitoba Harvest Hemp Foods,
    198–99
McMillan, Kristina, 160–61
mixed greens
    with hazelnut gomae, 18

roasted beet, gouda, and pickled
    onion salad, 168–70
Montreal Canadiens, 107
mujaddara, 143–44
mushrooms
    and bran risotto, 21
    stewed, with polenta and parsley
        salad, 38–40
    wild, and stinging nettle gnocchi,
        73–74
    wild leek and morel quiche, 148

n

Nature Conservancy of Canada, 77
NDG Food Depot, 152–53
Neal Brothers Foods, 85
nettles. *See* stinging nettles
New Farm, The, 84–85, 259, 260
New York Times Cook Book
    (Claiborne), 17
Niagara College, 258
noodles
    spicy pork, 135
NorWest Co-op Community Food
    Centre, 160–61
Not Far from the Tree, 182

o

oatmeal
    and leek biscuits, 57
Ocean Wise, 17, 212, 280
oils
    lime, 140
    paprika, 140
onions
    caramelized, perogies, 65–66

pickled, 170
Order of Canada, 93
Ottolenghi, Yotam, 224

p

Paganelli, Anna, 165
pancetta
  and chickpea soup, 132
paneer
  with spinach, tomatoes, and
    quinoa, 282
panna cotta, 151
paprika oil, 140
parsley
  salad, 38
parsnip
  and cauliflower soup, 230
  purée, 46
  root vegetable slaw, 224
  winter root mash, 197
pasta
  macaroni and cheese, 117
pears
  caramelized, 50–51
  poached in red wine, 165
Perigree, 69
PERL (Protecting Escarpment
  Rural Land), 250
perogies
  caramelized onion, 65–66
Perrin, Todd, 272–73
pesto
  and squash feta bake, 257
pickerel
  baked, with mango salsa, 162
pickles
  bread and butter, 70

pies, savoury
  crust, 252
  summer tomato tart, 260
  vegetable, 252–54
  wild leek and morel quiche, 148
Pizzeria Libretto, 242–43
polenta
  Don Valley pudding, 54
  with stewed mushrooms and
    parsley salad, 38–40
pork
  belly and crispy egg salad, 184–87
  side ribs soup, 120
  spicy noodles, 135
potato chips
  halibut crunch, 6
potatoes
  bacon rösti, 103–4
  caramelized onion perogies, 65–66
  and leek soup, 268
  rainbow vegetable curry, 32
  roasted, salad, 238
  wild mushroom and stinging
    nettle gnocchi, 65–67
  winter root mash, 197
Prager, Jenn, 112–13
Preston, Brent, 84
Pronto Restaurant, 52
Pull Together, 251

q

quiche
  wild leek and morel, 148
quinoa
  chicken salad, 129
  with spinach, tomatoes, and
    paneer, 282

r

radicchio
  grilled, with balsamic vinegar, 194
Raincity Grill, 17
Ramsay, Gordon, 183
Recipe for Change, 242
red snapper
  seafood chowder, 26
Regent Park Community Food Centre, 30, 59
Restaurant Makeover (TV show), 52
Restaurants for Change, 182, 228
Reynaud, Olivier, 228
rice
  arancini with mozzarella, 247–48
  burrito bowl, 159
rice balls (arancini), 247–48
rice bran
  broth, 21–22
  and mushroom risotto, 21–22
rice noodles
  spicy pork, 135
Richmond Station, 58–59
Ride with Rouge, 228
risotto
  barley, 174
  mushroom and bran, 21
Roberts, Sam, 85
Robin des Bois, 136–37
Rogalski, Paul, 228–29
Rosenfeld, Elana, 76–77
rösti
  bacon, with cheesy scrambled eggs, 103–94
Rouge et Noir, 228
Rouge Restaurant, 228–29

Ruby WatchCo., 182–83
rugelach
  caramel apple butter, 209–10
rum BBQ sauce, 277
Ryerson University, 125

s

salads. *See also* dressings, salad
  beet caprese, 244
  crispy egg and pork belly, 184–87
  parsley, 38
  quinoa chicken, 129
  roasted beet, gouda, and pickled onion, 168–70
  roasted potato, 238
  root vegetable slaw, 224
  spicy slaw, 158
salmon
  marinated wild sockeye, 100
  rillettes, 111
  seafood chowder, 26
salsa, 159
  mango, 162
sandwiches
  chicken, 241
sauces, savoury
  homestyle butter, 285
  mango salsa, 162
  rum BBQ, 277
  salsa, 159
sauces, sweet
  crème anglaise, 51
Saul, Nick, 42, 68, 69, 119, 124, 146, 222–23
Scaramouche, 146–47
Scarborough Hospital, 125

scones
    Rocky Mountain, 78
seafood. *See also* fish
    chowder, 26
    Dungeness crab tacos, 214–16
    shrimp curry, 35
Seed Winnipeg, 36
Servay, Judy, 136–37
sherry vinaigrette, 234
shrimp
    curry, 35
Sole Food, 193
Sooke Harbour House, 17
soups
    chickpea and pancetta, 132
    dahl, 138–40
    mujaddara, 143–44
    potato leek, 268
    roasted cauliflower and parsnip,
      230
    seafood chowder, 26
    side ribs, 120
    turkey chowder, 114
Soup Siblings, 267
Soup Sisters/Broth Brothers, 266–67
Soupstock, 251
spinach
    sautéed, with tomatoes, quinoa,
      and paneer, 282
Springsteen, Bruce, 229
squash
    chickpea and pancetta soup, 132
    pesto feta bake, 257
    rainbow vegetable curry, 32
Stadtlander, Michael, 146
stinging nettles
    and wild mushroom gnocchi,
      73–74
Stop, The, 42, 43, 85, 146, 176–77,
    223, 237

Stop Community Food Centre, The,
    68, 69, 118, 124, 242, 258–59, 260
Stratford Chefs School, 58
Street Farm (Ableman), 193
Streiman, Miriam, 204–5
Sunburst Farms, 192
SuperChefs of the Universe, 25
Sustainability/Growers/Green
    Initiatives Committee, 17
Suzuki, David, 166, 250
sweet potato
    burrito bowl, 157–59
    rainbow vegetable curry, 32
    roasted, 157–58

t

Table Community Food Centre,
    130–31
tacos
    Dungeness crab, 214–16
Taylor, Paul, 236–37
Tempered Chef, The, 42–43
360 (restaurant), 52
tomatoes
    chickpea and pancetta soup, 132
    homestyle butter sauce, 285
    ketchup, 274
    salsa, 159
    smoky chakchouka, 154
    with spinach, quinoa, and
      paneer, 282
    summer tart, 260
Top Chef Canada (TV show), 58, 273
Toronto Food Policy Council, 52
Tragically Hip, The, 85
trout
    bourguignon, 60
truffle jus, 47

turkey
   chowder, 114
   enchilada pie, 9

u

University of British Columbia, 280, 281
University of Winnipeg, 36–37

v

Vancouver Food Policy Council, 237
vegetables
   rainbow curry, 32
   root, slaw, 224
   savoury pie, 252–54
   squash pesto feta bake, 257
Vij, Vikram, 280–81

Vij's Kitchen, 281
vinaigrettes
   apple cider, 170
   Brown Derby, 187
   honey and lime, 214
   sherry, 234
   white balsamic, 244

w

Walker, Ian, 92–93
wonton taco shells, 214
Wooden Monkey, The, 166–67
World Culinary Olympics, 24

y

Yorkshire Valley Farms, 259

good food changes lives

Food is this incredible thing. If you eat it together, you grow community and connection. Through it you can express your culture and your background. If you eat good food it energizes you and keeps you healthy. When you grow food sustainably, it nourishes the soil and increases the health of our planet. And when everyone has access to good food, you have inclusive, connected, and equitable communities.

—Nick Saul, President & CEO,
Community Food Centres Canada

50% of the profits from the sale of

goodness: recipes & stories

will be donated to **Community Food Centres Canada** to bring people in low-income communities together to grow, cook, share, and advocate for healthy food for all.

Find out more at **cfccanada.ca** and **nealbrothersfoods.com/goodness**